CW00666015

SLAUGHTER
IN THE
STREETS

SLAUGHTER IN THE STREETS

WHEN BOSTON BECAME BOXING'S MURDER CAPITAL

DON STRADLEY

FOREWORD BY T. J. ENGLISH
AUTHOR OF PADDY WHACKED

HAMILCAR NOIR

HARD-HITTING TRUE CRIME

ISBN: 978-1-949590-25-8

Publisher's Cataloging-in-Publication Data
Names: Stradley, Don, author.
Title: Slaughter in the streets : when Boston became boxing's murder capital / Don Stradley.
Series: Hamilcar Noir
Description: Includes bibliographical references. | Boston, MA: Hamilcar Publications
Identifiers: LCCN 2019953176 | ISBN 9781949590258
Subjects: LCSH Boxing—Massachusetts—Boston. | Boxing—Massachusetts—Boston—History—20th century. | Organized crime—Massachusetts—Boston. | Boston (Mass.)—History—20th century. | Boxing—Corrupt practices—United States—History. | BISAC SPORTS & RECREATION / Boxing | TRUE CRIME / Organized Crime | HISTORY / United States / State & Local / New England (CT, MA, ME, NH, RI, VT)
Classification: LCC GV1136.5.S77 2020 | DDC 796.830973–dc23

Hamilcar Publications
An imprint of Hannibal Boxing Media
Ten Post Office Square, 8th Floor South
Boston, MA 02109
www.hamilcarpubs.com

Printed in the United States of American

On the cover: Eddie Connors shot dead in a Dorchester telephone booth. *The Boston Globe/Getty Images*

Frontispiece: Joe Barboza testifies before the House Crime Committee in Washington, DC, in 1972. *Bettman Archive/Getty Images*

For all the boxers . . . and for all the criminals

CONTENTS

They died violently in a multitude of ways: beat to death with a pipe or a lead sash weight wrapped in newspaper; shot point-blank in the face with a .38 revolver; pistol whipped, then shot in the head; strangled with bailing wire; stabbed to death with a butcher knife; shot in the balls and in the chest with a pump-action shotgun; behind the ear with a small-caliber handgun; in the stomach; shot in the back and then asphyxiated with a trash bag pulled tight over the head; shot on the street, in saloons, behind the wheel of a car, in a phone booth in the dead of night; shot in the temple and left floating in the Mystic River, hands and feet bound together with wire; bodies left in car trunks, on the side of the road, in the gutter.

A sane person would rightfully conclude that these were ignominious endings. Certainly, it is not the way you would want a loved one to ride out their final hours on earth.

Some might say, and did say, that these men got what they deserved. Most of them had crossed over to the dark side and were involved in crime: petty larceny, illegal gambling, fencing stolen goods, narcotics, burglary, murder—you name it. Some of these men were used and manipulated by high-level gangsters and Mafiosi. To coin a phrase, they lived by the sword and died by the sword. They were the embodiment of that old-school term "palooka," a loser, of sorts, whose life seems destined for a brutal demise.

That these men were wayward souls is hard to deny, but they were also once somebody's little boy, somebody's brother, uncle, or father. All of them started out with a dream, which was to rise up out of humble circumstances—out of the gutter—and find fame and glory through the sport of boxing.

The historical fact that the city of Boston has seen more than its share of this breed—boxers who became intertwined with the criminal underworld—is the literary gold that author Don Stradley mines so beautifully in this book. There are moments of triumph in the ring, and some failures; Stradley is right to focus as much on the boxing careers (often misbegotten) of these men as well as their criminal associations and habits. They lived hard lives and died horrible deaths, and some might even surmise that their lives are better off forgotten. But even the lowliest of lives has much to reveal to us about the city in which these men toiled.

A few years back, in the summer of 2013, I had the occasion to attend the duration of gangster boss Whitey Bulger's criminal trial in the city. The proceedings took place at the Moakley Courthouse in the Seaport District. The Seaport was once home to the city's thriving commercial waterfront, where more than a few of the men profiled in this book found work as longshoremen and union "delegates" (i.e., leg breakers for the International Longshoremen's Association).

At the time of the trial, the area had already begun its startling transformation from a hardscrabble workingman's environment to the conglomeration of high-rise condos, glass office towers and chic restaurants that it is today.

Gentrification can be a brutal process. It does not involve snub-nosed revolvers, lead pipes, or switchblade knives, but it does involve wholesale displacement of poor and working people, unnatural alterations of the landscape, the destruction of lives. One man's economic development is another's predatory capitalism.

Few would disagree that the Seaport District—and the city of Boston—is not better off than it was during the historical era that this book so vibrantly evokes. Even so, it is useful to remember that the ground beneath these glistening new condos and office towers is saturated with the blood of those who came before, men who lived and died in a city known for its hard-nosed working-class, rough-and-tumble politics and pitiless criminal underworld. In many ways, the lives lived by this oddball collection of palookas laid the foundation for the thriving international city that Boston is today.

Their legacy, as detailed in *Slaughter in the Streets*, is in the air we breathe. Their DNA, quite literally, is embedded in the soil beneath our feet.

T. J. English
New York City
September 2019

Bad choices put them all in early graves.
They died violently and stupidly, in a Boston that no longer exists.

They'd been fighters.
They thought bullets were nothing to fear.
They thought their toughness in the ring would help them survive
on the street.

Their deaths made headlines.
But they remained small players in a story much bigger than their own.

They deserve to be brought to the front of the story,
to be pulled out of the background and prepared for their close-ups.
Their tales should be told.

Just once.

The end of the Gustin Gang: Frankie "Gustin" ambushed on Hanover Street in Boston's North End. *Courtesy of the Boston Public Library, Leslie Jones Collection*

CHAPTER 1

The Shooting Gallery

Guns, Knives, and Desperate Lives . . .

He was one hell of a criminal, but he'd never been much of a fighter.

That was the word on Frankie Wallace, a South Boston flyweight who made his professional ring debut on September 25, 1922. Frankie's older brother Stevie had been a featherweight of some renown, earning a place on the 1920 U.S. Olympic team and taking part in thirty-five professional bouts. But Frankie, as the cops would later say, wasn't quite as "hard-boiled" as Stevie. He ended up losing his first pro start to another local kid, Jimmy Manning. The humiliating defeat inspired Frankie's buddies to appear at Manning's house the next day. They beat him senseless. This resulted in a prolonged series of street skirmishes all around Southie.

Frankie Wallace became better known as Frankie Gustin, leader of South Boston's notorious Gustin Gang. By the time he was thirty, Frankie's group of Irish American thugs had become famous during the Prohibition era for robbing liquor trucks. Frankie became such a big player in the city's underworld that his eventual murder in 1931 was one of Boston's biggest stories of the year. It also shaped the city's crime landscape for decades to come.

Frankie had always been a riddle to the police. He was soft-spoken and friendly, though he had a steep record of arrests, was a suspect in at least one murder, and was on the verge of forming his own criminal empire. The Gustins, so named after a street in Southie, developed such a reputation that they began to irritate Boston's growing Italian Mob. The breaking point came when Frankie's gang wanted control of all bootlegging along Boston's waterfront, which had previously been wide open. The Gustins had even robbed a few trucks that had been targeted by the Italians. This was an example of the Irish gang's increasing arrogance. And it was bad news for Frankie.

Two days before Christmas of 1931, Frankie arrived in Boston's North End to discuss how the local booze trade could be divided between the Gustins and the Italians. He showed up with two of his sidekicks, including Bernard "Dodo" Walsh, a twenty-four-year-old described by police as "just a punk and a gun-toter." The meeting was held on the third floor of 317 Hanover Street in the office of C and F Importers, allegedly where Mob "underboss" Joseph Lombardo oversaw his own bootlegging operation. Frankie should've been wary. The area was so known for gunplay that neighborhood cops had dubbed it "the shooting gallery." On the fourth floor, a charity group wrapped Christmas baskets for poor children of the North End. The roar of gunfire soon startled them. Frankie and Dodo had been ambushed and killed.

Frankie spent the final seconds of his life the way James Cagney might've in an old Warner Brothers crime drama—he stumbled down the hallway and into the office of an attorney who had leased space in the building. A female stenographer who had been filling out Christmas cards looked on in horror; the sound of guns a moment earlier had shattered the holiday mood, and now she was confronted by the sight of Frankie in the doorway, blood gushing from his wounds. Without saying a word, he walked in. Then he pitched forward, dead.

He landed awkwardly, his head wedged into the under-railings of a wooden chair. As Frankie bled out on the attorney's floor, so went his plans to dominate the waterfront.

The story was a sensation. Boston police fanned out as far north as Portland, Maine, in search of Lombardo and his men, while *The Boston Globe* built up Frankie as a little terror who had dominated the local crime scene "with a grip of steel." Also played up was the seemingly minor detail of how Frankie and his brother "fought within the squared circle."

One had to wonder if Frankie's life would've been different had he been victorious in his first and only professional fight. Would he have pursued boxing, or would he still have gone into crime? Then again, Stevie was very successful in the ring, and his taste for robbing was just as developed as Frankie's. Maybe crime and boxing were in them in equal parts. Maybe it was inevitable that one of them would be killed in a North End gun battle. After all, Boston already had a history of fighters being killed gangland style.

The boxer gunned down by gangsters may be a fixture of old movies, but it is not a myth. The melodrama of a desperate fighter pursued by seedy killers, the crack of gunfire, the bullet-riddled corpse dumped in a secluded area; these situations were not solely the work of screenwriters during Hollywood's Golden Age. They were rooted in truth.

Of course, these murders weren't very cinematic. They rarely, if ever, had anything to do with fixed fights, and the murdered boxer would be familiar to only the most astute fans of the fight game. A famous fighter wouldn't let himself get sucked into this kind of trouble. Instead, it was the fighter on the fringe of the business, the preliminary kid, who found himself staring down a gun barrel or, as was usually the case, shot behind the ear.

Just six months before Frankie Gustin's murder, the body of East Boston pugilist Jerry DiAngelis turned up in Chelsea. He'd been shot to death and left in a wooded area known as a gangland dumping ground. Prior to that was the 1925 murder of former boxer Johnny Vito, a North Ender whose corpse was found in Braintree, face down in mud. The murderer remained unknown, though police believed Vito had been killed trying to hijack a liquor truck. In December of 1915, a shady character named Joseph Damico was found stabbed to death in an East Boston alley. The *Globe* savored every gash, noting Damico was "struck on the neck, the blow severing the jugular vein and nearly cutting through the spine." Damico, who had fought more than twenty times as "Tommy Young," turned out to be an unsavory character with gang connections in New York. Rivaling Gustin's death for coverage was the February 1929 murder of North Ender Anthony "Sparky" Chiampa. Nineteen-year-old Sparky was found dead in a Revere barn, bullet holes in the back of his head and under each eye.

Though he hadn't turned professional, Chiampa was known for boxing at various athletic clubs around the city, and the news coverage of his murder made several references to him as "the little fighter." Boxing, even at the amateur level, was a major North End attraction during the 1920s. The sport had flourished throughout the world, but the Italian Americans of Boston's North End believed their boys were as good and tough as anyone. North End lightweight Sabino Ferullo, who took the name "Sammy Fuller" and became the most popular Italian fighter in Boston, would give away a hundred tickets to the neighborhood children; they showed up at his fights with trumpets and bugles, blaring away as he punched his opponents. For North Enders, boxing was as much a celebration of Italian life as the annual Saint Anthony's Feast in June, which is partly why Chiampa's murder hit Boston like a hammer.

Like many of the city's young men, Chiampa dabbled in crime. At the time of his death he was scheduled to appear in court to testify against some of his cronies. It was also believed that he'd recently robbed a dice game on Friend Street and hadn't shared the loot with his partners. Investigators had dozens of theories and suspects, but no one was ever charged with Chiampa's murder.

The killing of Chiampa was especially ominous. There'd been no signs of robbery, and his murderer hadn't even bothered to remove an expensive diamond ring from his hand; he was killed solely to shut him up, to keep him from talking in court. It was an event described in one newspaper as "the first real introduction of Chicago gang warfare into Boston."

But it was the ambush of Frankie Gustin that was drilled into the minds of rough kids who grew up in the post-Depression neighborhoods of the North End and East Boston, which were predominantly Italian, and South Boston and Charlestown, which were mostly Irish. Those neighborhoods, wrote the *Globe* more than six decades later, "spawned most of the city's gangsters, who carried ethnic-based animosities like chips on their shoulders."

Simultaneously, Gustin's murder was part of a second story playing out, that of a boxer being murdered in Boston. It is an unusual status to claim, but few cities can match Boston for its number of slain fighters. Of the more than three hundred and fifty professional and amateur fighters murdered worldwide since Gustin's death in 1931, a shocking amount of those killings took place in Boston and its neighboring towns. Most were gang related. Many were unsolved.

Frankie's brother Stevie stepped in as the gang's new leader, but within ten years the Gustins were considered relics of the Prohibition age. However, their work was already done. They had established a criminal archetype. Cocky, brash, and daring, they were forerunners of the South Boston criminals to come, the poor, scrappy Irish boys who emerged from the worst parts of Southie to embark on unlawful careers. The most notorious, of course, was James "Whitey" Bulger, who in his early days was simply another Southie hood following the template of the Gustins. Yet he would become America's most famous criminal and turn the Boston FBI into his partners. When the FBI eventually brought down the city's Italian Mob in the 1980s, it was with Whitey's help. Before he was done, Bulger would wield a kind of influence that would've been unimaginable to the boys on Gustin Street.

And fifty years after the Gustins, boxers were still playing a part in the Boston crime scene. Bulger never had more than a passing interest in boxing, but he certainly used local fighters as henchmen. More than one of his boxing flunkies landed in prison for an extended stay. In 1975, Bulger and an accomplice decided they couldn't trust a retired local middleweight named Eddie Connors. They shot him to bits in a phone booth and created a scene as gory as anything from the old Hanover Street shooting gallery. Connors, who had boxed many times at the Boston Garden, made the mistake of getting too familiar with his criminal pals. For his trouble, he was cut nearly in half by a carbine and left to soak in his own blood.

As for Joseph Lombardo, he was acquitted in connection to the Gustin murder and went on for many years as the North End's underboss. During the 1950s and 60s, Lombardo served as consigliere for a new generation of mobsters, namely the Patriarca crime family in Providence, and was a mentor to Boston's new underboss, Gennaro "Jerry" Angiulo. In the years before his death in 1969, when he was an elderly restaurant owner, Lombardo still commanded respect. Even the craziest young soldiers of the city's new Mafia knew that "J. L." had stopped the Gustins.

The murder of Frankie Gustin established a long-term understanding that the Irish crooks and the Mafia would coexist in the city as separate but not quite equal entities. At times they'd work together. At times they would be at war. Boston's criminal world was complicated, always evolving, often confusing. And Frankie, the failed flyweight, wouldn't be the last fighter caught in the crossfire.

Boston was on its way to becoming boxing's murder capital.

Phil Buccola.

Phil Buccola:
Boston's Beloved Mob Boss

*The Only Thing He Loved More Than Boxing
Was Crime . . .*

According to local gangster lore, the murder of Frankie Gustin had been ordered by Boston's top Italian crime boss, Filippo "Phil" Buccola (aka "Bruccola" or "Buccalo"). Quiet and pleasant, Buccola was one of the Mafia's best-kept secrets. He'd come to America from Palermo, and with the stealth of a small jungle lizard managed to stay invisible, even in plain sight. Rather than do business in some badly lit waterfront shack, he was out among the people. With his thinning hair and wire-rimmed spectacles, he looked more like a pharmacist than a mobster.

The 1933 killing of Jewish bootlegger and drug trafficker Charles "King" Solomon was also attributed to Buccola. A compelling version of the story has Buccola hiring the remaining members of the Gustins to kill Solomon, though some believe Solomon's death was just a robbery gone wrong. Then again, the murder of Solomon took place at a nightclub owned by Dan Carroll, an ex-cop who happened to be Buccola's partner in many business ventures.

With the city's top Irish and Jewish gangsters bumped off, Buccola seized the Boston underworld. He wasn't as bloodthirsty as his counterparts in

New York or Chicago, but his clique was clearly Mafia, with rites and roots going back to feudal Sicily. It was later revealed that Buccola was also quite friendly with Charles "Lucky" Luciano, the man who introduced America to the concept of the organized crime "family."

Though Buccola owned shares in a popular dog-racing track in Revere and a piece of The Bostonian Hotel, his real interest was boxing. He was known as a manager of fighters, sometimes alone, sometimes with Carroll or another well-known manager, Johnny Buckley. It wasn't unusual for top gangsters to own a fighter's contract the way they might a racehorse or a restaurant, but Buccola took the fight game seriously. He had a full stable of New England fighters, most of them from the North End. At one time there were as many as twenty-five fighters under the Buccola banner, including North Ender Sammy Fuller and Ralph "The Ripper" Zannelli, a granite-faced welterweight from Providence. But despite Buccola's genuine passion for boxing, he was, according to one journalist, "rated by colleagues as one of the world's worst fight handlers."

Like most managers in those days, Buccola's dream was to find a good heavyweight. Specifically, he wanted a heavyweight of Italian ancestry. By 1929 there were whispers out of New York that a team of mobsters and Broadway shills had purchased the contract of Primo Carnera, a former circus strongman who would, with some help behind the scenes, eventually become heavyweight champion. Perhaps not coincidentally, when Carnera came to Rhode Island in 1932 for the only time in his career, he fought one of Buccola's fighters, an aging journeyman named Jack Gagnon. Buccola's man lost at 1:35 of the first round. As was often the case with Carnera's bouts, the ending seemed highly suspicious. Gagnon went down from a tap and wouldn't move, even as the spectators hooted. According to the Associated Press, "Carnera stood with a surprised look on his face until he was announced the victor."

Determined to find his own Carnera, Buccola began importing fighters from Italy. The most widely publicized was a hairy hulk named Riccardo

Bertazzolo. But after Bertazzolo lost seven fights in a row—including a third-round knockout loss to Carnera in Atlantic City—Buccola shipped him back to Europe.

Buccola's partner in bringing Bertazzolo to America was Frank Marlow, a high-rolling New York gambler, club owner, and fight manager. Just weeks after Bertazzolo's arrival, Marlow was found shot to death in a Queens gutter. Marlow's murder went unsolved, but there were plenty of lively suspects, including New York racketeer "Joe the Boss" Masseria and former middleweight champion Johnny Wilson of Boston, allegedly angry that Marlow owed him money. Even Buccola was wanted for questioning.

Buccola's shady side wasn't a secret. His rap sheet included a 1923 weapons charge and a bust for taking part in an illegal lottery operation. In 1935, he was charged with tax fraud. By 1947, authorities suspected Buccola was not only a high-powered racketeer, but that his reach extended all the way to Providence. Still, Italians throughout Boston had great admiration for Buccola. He wasn't merely a mobster; he was also available to give advice on anything from domestic problems to business investments. In the 1930s and 40s, Italians in Boston still faced prejudice and couldn't always find assistance in the accepted manner. As future welterweight champion Tony DeMarco once put it, "When we couldn't go to the police or to our local congressman, we went to someone like Phil Buccola."

By 1950, Buccola was on the radar of Estes Kefauver, a Tennessee senator out to smash organized crime. In 1954, weary of federal investigations and the Internal Revenue Service, Buccola returned to Sicily. When Mafia rat Joe Valachi spilled his guts in 1963 about the inner workings of the Mob, he informed the FBI that Buccola had indeed been La Cosa Nostra's top man in Massachusetts, possibly in all of New England, and that his underworld resume included extortion and murder. By the time Valachi squealed, Buccola was living in Sicily as a chicken farmer. He lived to be 101 years old.

The generation of Boston boys who grew up during Buccola's reign saw an unmistakable link between boxing and crime. They saw that gangsters like Buccola were revered. Boxers had followings, but gangsters had real clout and were the unmistakable stars of the neighborhood. When North End gangster Carmelo Giuffre was slain in January of 1931, so many mourners crammed the Charter Street home where his body was on view that the second-floor hallway began collapsing; the fire department arrived to keep the stream of visitors down to groups of five.

The adoration of gangsters was such a growing concern that Dr. A. Z. Conrad, the powerhouse pastor at Boston's Park Street Congregational Church, addressed the issue in a March 1932 radio address on WHDH. "The reason that so many boys almost worship gangsters is because we have made heroes of the gangster and the racketeer," Conrad said. Known for his finger-wagging sermons from Boston's "Brimstone Corner," Conrad blamed "the infernal moving pictures" that "presented crime in an attractive form." But Boston's kids didn't need to go to the movies to see gangsters. The bad guys were right there in the neighborhood.

By Buccola's era, the Italian American mobster was undergoing a change of image. They were no longer old-country types operating under the cloak of darkness and hiding their money in a mattress. They were increasingly Americanized. They understood the city's politics and knew how to manipulate the local power structures. If they indulged in criminal activity, the reasoning went, it was only because American society had yet to fully embrace the Italians. Legit jobs were scarce; a fellow made a buck where he could. An elegant, intelligent man such as Buccola wasn't to be lumped in with the Black Handers, narcotics dealers, or two-bit robbers. If the authorities ever accused Buccola of anything too sinister, his admirers simply wouldn't believe it.

As boxing fever swept the city in the 1930s and 40s, Boston's underworld grew as well. In this dangerously charged atmosphere, it was inevitable that the city's boxers would intertwine with gangsters. Not surprisingly, there was an uptick in the number of local fighters getting whacked. The most famous of them was Nate Siegel, a popular welterweight from Revere who had twice fought the legendary Mickey Walker. In 1934, an assassin shot Siegel to death in his own home. Siegel owned a tavern and was believed to have come between rival liquor distributors, but no one was ever charged with his murder.

There were others: George Brogna, who fought as "Johnny DeLano," was a twenty-six-year-old East Boston featherweight with a record of 12-9-5. He'd also been deeply involved in gangland activity and had allegedly killed a local bootlegger, "Big Mike" Richardi (who had been suspected of killing Johnny Vito). In 1933, Brogna's body was found in Revere. He'd been beaten about the head and shot three times. That same year saw the murder of Joseph Wolf, a petty criminal with gang ties who fought as "Charley 'KO' Elkins." His ring resume was 15-9-2, plus seventy-two arrests and eleven appeals. He was found dead on a South End sidewalk. It was believed that the owner of a local barroom had killed him. Wolf, a thirty-four-year-old still living with his mother on Harrison Avenue, had tried to shake the owner down for "protection" money. Big mistake.

In December of 1937, David "Beano" Breen, a former boxer who became a big name in the Boston rackets, was fatally shot in the lobby of the Metropolitan Hotel on Tremont Street. In March of 1939, Patrick J. "Paddy" Flynn died after being shot in a Malden gambling house. Ironically, Flynn had been an opponent of Nate Siegel. Siegel beat Flynn three times, but they both ended up dead, Siegel by shotgun, Flynn courtesy of a .22-caliber slug in the brain.

Chiampa. DiAngelis. Wallace. Brogna. Wolf. Siegel. Breen. Flynn. Eight fighters killed in ten years. The police occasionally found an abandoned weapon, but few arrests were made. The killers seemed to vanish like one of those cloaked gunmen in an old-time radio serial.

All of these fighters were involved in liquor, gambling, and extortion. Is it a coincidence that they were working in the domain of Phil Buccola?

There is a terrible irony here, in that the Mob boss who purportedly loved boxing may have known at least a few of these doomed fighters, may have watched them train, may have spoken to them. And he may have played a part in some of their murders.

One never knew exactly what was going on with Buccola. In a city filled with slick operators, he was probably the slickest.

Promoter Sam Silverman and Muhammad Ali in
Boston, 1965. *AP Photo*

CHAPTER 3

Boxing Booms in Boston

But Killers Never Rest . . .

n July of 1944, in between reports about the Normandy invasion, Bostonians read that another local fighter had been killed in the city. Vincent "Pepper" Martin, who had been born as Yaparan Alajajian, was found dead in a car on Ipswich Street in Back Bay. He had fifty bucks in his pocket and a bullet in each lung.

A South End bookie with a record of carrying unregistered guns and passing counterfeit bills, Martin had served eighteen months at Deer Island for shooting a woman, and had once attacked his ex-wife with a knife. Martin was also known as a smirking punk who liked to flash big wads of money. Certain his murder was linked to his gambling habit, police began rounding up a local gang known for sticking up dice games.

Though he'd had only a handful of fights, newspapers placed heavy focus on Martin's boxing background. More was made of Martin's boxing career than the fact that he'd once stabbed his ex-wife in the head.

The killing of Pepper Martin was front-page material. As America was learning from the movies, fighters attracted a certain undesirable element. Hence, the murder of a fighter made for an easy, attention-grabbing headline. Then again, a fighter didn't have to be killed to make news. They were increasingly involved in tawdry scenes, and Boston papers couldn't get enough headlines about the city's boxers behaving badly. Stories rolled out of the *Globe* with almost comical frequency: "Hub Divorcee Held in Slaying of Ex-Boxer," "Ex-Boxer Runs Amok, Killed by Patrolman," "Ex-Pugilist Sought for Taxi-Cab Murder," "Former Boxer Held for Assault on Revere Mayor," "Ex-Boxer in Cell for Safe-Keeping," "Ex-Boxer Sentenced in Narcotics Case," "Hub Ex-Boxer Gets Year for Probation Break," "Ex-Boxer Wants Sentence Cut But Won't Talk," "$40,000 Bail Set for Ex-Boxer in Extortion Plot," "Bullet Misses West End Boxer; Manager Held," "Trio Under Arrest for Beating of Boxer," "Ex-Boxer Gets 18–20 Years in Woman's Death."

Even if a fellow had boxed only a few times in the amateurs or in the Navy, the term "ex-boxer" was jammed into these gruesome stories as often as possible. A mere thirty years later, the opposite would be true. When Leon Easterling fatally stabbed Harvard football star Andrew Puopolo in Boston's Combat Zone in 1976, Easterling's past as a professional boxer was never mentioned in the media's massive coverage of that case—but in the 1940s, the term had juice. The term conjured up stinking gyms, smoky arenas, violence, gambling, and a hint of corruption. Newsroom editors never hesitated to exploit boxing's dark and degenerate aura, especially since the sport had thrived in Boston during the war years.

Though the rest of the country noticed a drop in boxing attendance during the war, Boston promoters observed a sudden spike in ticket sales. New York remained the premier boxing city, but Boston enjoyed an unexpected wartime boom. Stars such as Sugar Ray Robinson, Fritzie Zivic, Ike Williams, and Henry Armstrong began to fight there with regularity Featherweight champion Willie Pep came to Boston twice in 1943 to fight East Boston's great featherweight Sal Bartolo. Even heavyweight champion Joe Louis, the most revered fighter in the world, arrived in Boston in December of 1940 to beat Al McCoy at the Garden. From 1942 to 1945, the city hosted an average of one boxing show per week, a chaotic pace that would never again be matched.

Boston venues could actually draw a near sellout with nothing but homegrown talent. Tommy Collins, a modestly gifted lightweight from Medford, became a certified star in Boston, while Tony DeMarco—short, awkward, with a blood sugar problem that caused him to fall apart in the late rounds—emerged from Fleet Street in the North End to win the city's heart. (The trick to being a local success, of course, was to be Irish or Italian. African American fighters were a harder sell.)

When DeMarco (real name Leonardo Liotta) defeated Johnny Saxton for the welterweight championship in 1955, a cavalcade of Boston boys took up boxing. According to local aficionados, there was a period of time when Clark Street in the North End was the address of no less than eight professional fighters.

The city's growing success as a boxing market was due largely to the efforts of two men, Sam Silverman and Anthony "Rip" Valenti. Silverman, who had been promoting fights since the 1930s, was not without enemies. In 1951, a bullet ripped through a window of his Chelsea home. In 1954, someone rigged Silverman's house with a bomb. It was thought that Silverman was being targeted because he wouldn't submit to national matchmakers wanting to control the sport. As he shuffled through the broken glass and debris in his living room, he told reporters it hadn't been a bomb but merely a defective refrigerator. In 1968, Silverman found himself in court defending himself against charges of bribing an undercard fighter to take a dive; the case ended in a mistrial.

As for Valenti, he'd been part of the Phil Buccola–Dan Carroll–Johnny Buckley era. At various times he was a matchmaker, an agent, a discoverer of talent, a gadfly, and a promoter. Because of his police record he spent many years without an official manager's license; he compensated by guiding a fighter's career from a backroom and using local men as fronts. By the time of his death at age eighty-three in 1986, Valenti had become a treasured local character, partly because he presented himself

SLAUGHTER IN THE STREETS

as an old-time operator at odds with a constantly changing world. As the *Globe* noted, Valenti "always looked sad because of his big eyes and drooping lids."

But sad old Valenti had a stronger hand than anyone realized.

"Rip was well connected," said Jerry Forte, a North End fighter who later served as the state's assistant boxing commissioner. "He was tight with Joe Lombardo, who was Buccola's right-hand man." This, according to Forte, was why New York managers or promoters could never snatch a Boston fighter from Valenti's grasp.

"The New York Mob wouldn't touch Rip," Forte said. "There was an incident where a New Yorker tried to take one of Rip's fighters; Rip went to New York and had a meeting with some people. That was the end of that. There was respect for Rip in that way."

Valenti was also known to be a friend of Frankie Carbo, the former Mafia gunman who controlled much of the boxing landscape in the 1950s. For his part, Valenti played dumb. In 1982, the *Globe* asked him about the Mob's impact on boxing. "Organized crime has nothing to do with boxing," he said. "What does organized crime need with boxing, anyway?" As for Carbo, Valenti shrugged. "Carbo was all right. He used to help me make matches."

Valenti could deny that the Mob had anything to do with boxing, but when Ted Williams had trouble with Red Sox brass, he didn't consult the local Mafia boss. Consider the way Valenti and DeMarco once dealt with a problem.

Near the end of his career, DeMarco wanted to break from Valenti and manage himself. Since Phil Buccola was no longer in the city, DeMarco sought out advice from Raymond Patriarca, the ruthless crime boss who had replaced Buccola as New England's Mafia kingpin. Like characters from *The Godfather*, DeMarco and Valenti journeyed to Patriarca's Providence office bearing tributes—Cuban cigars, North End cannoli—and explained their cases. Patriarca, who probably had more pressing issues to consider, squinted at the pair through a cloud of Cuban cigar smoke. He politely told DeMarco to stay with Valenti for three more fights. DeMarco claimed to be happy with the edict, but it's not as if he would argue with Patriarca. It's safe to say Valenti probably benefited from his old Mob ties to get DeMarco for three more bouts. But according to Valenti, the Mob had nothing to do with boxing. (And according to DeMarco, Patriarca was just a businessman.)

Boston's run as a successful boxing market continued until the establishment of the International Boxing Club in 1949. The IBC, headed by James Norris with Carbo as his unofficial matchmaker and "convincer," quickly grabbed the contracts of the day's top fighters, tied up television coverage, and brought fights to New York, or to cities where the wealthy Norris owned pieces of venues. Boston was out of the IBC loop. (That a few marquee names fought DeMarco in Boston has been attributed to Valenti's connection to Carbo.) In 1957, Silverman cited an illegal restraint of trade and sued the IBC for nine million dollars. The out-of-court settlement—for much less than nine million dollars—made Silverman look like a tough businessman but didn't help Boston in terms of hosting important fights.

The courts eventually dissolved the IBC, but former IBC president Truman Gibson told Senate investigators in 1960 that the Boston trio of Silverman, Valenti, and Johnny Buckley had been under Carbo's control all along. The stunned trio insisted their interaction with the former Mob killer was minimal, but Gibson's bombshell had made their reputations wobble. They recovered, but despite the dismantling of the IBC, Boston continued to struggle. By the late 1960s, Boston had dried up as a major fight town.

One thing that didn't change was the continuous melding of boxers and wise guys. You could tell where fighters stood in the Mob's pecking order by the jobs they were given: driver, bodyguard, doorman at a Mob restaurant. What brought so many of Boston's fighters into the criminal life? Was it because boxing itself requires a certain cold-bloodedness, which translates well to gangland activities? Was it unavoidable in a compact city such as Boston? When asked how it was so easy for these fighters to get involved with criminals, retired New England welterweight Eddie Grenke said simply, "neighborhood friends."

Eddie Spence, a popular Boston fighter of the 1960s, recalled a rather dark element that hovered around the boxing scene: "I would see semiliterate criminal types around the gyms," he said. "I remember a fellow who claimed to be Silverman's friend. Out of the blue he tells me that he has a beef with some guys. Then he shows me a handgun. He says, 'I plan to get them before they get me.' My manager told me to relax, but I was looking for the escape hatch."

In those secretive Boston enclaves, it grew increasingly difficult to tell the fighters from the felons. Sometimes you didn't know about a fighter's secret life until he got killed. That was the case in 1953 when old-time featherweight Morris "Whitey" Hurwitz was murdered outside his house in Brookline. Hurwitz, who had been a bodyguard for underworld figures, had his hand in everything from bookmaking to crooked dice games.

Then there was the savage 1955 murder of Fall River welterweight Al Frias. A rarity among New England's murdered fighters, twenty-six-year-old Frias was actually killed in New York. His body was found in a ditch beside Route 210. A fighter of minor talents—he'd lost several fights in a row and was in trouble with the Massachusetts commission for competing with an expired license—he'd been staying at a Manhattan hotel, frantically writing notes to his family back home that he'd come into some money. It was later learned that Frias was in New York on a mission to acquire $20,000 in counterfeit bills. Working for a "New England syndicate," Frias was to pay a couple of creeps $6,000 for the $20,000. His contacts changed their minds, robbed him, and shot him in the head.

The defendants in the case, George Ruocco and Joseph Marsala, claimed their confessions were made only after being brutalized by police. Despite this, they were found guilty of murder and sent to Sing Sing. Meanwhile, medical examiners couldn't figure out why there was a bullet hole in Frias's skull, but no exit wound and no slug found in his head. It was eventually determined that the bullet had fallen into his nasal cavity and dropped out of his mouth.

Pepper Martin? The newspapers went on and on about his boxing career, how on the last night of his life he was with the old North End slugger, Sammy Fuller, and how the two went to Braves Field to see Willie Pep fight Manuel Ortiz. Ironically, one of the suspects in Martin's murder was another ex-boxer, a Roxbury heavyweight named Jack McCarthy. McCarthy was exonerated but later served a prison term for illegal possession of a gun. The Martin murder was soon forgotten. He was buried in a cemetery in Watertown, a quiet suburb not known for boxers or killers.

Tommy Sullivan's murder was never solved.

Tommy Sullivan:
Everybody's Pal

*He Was a Hero in South Boston, but Someone
Wanted Him Dead . . .*

Tommy Sullivan's head was bleeding. He was on the floor of Jimmy O'Keefe's Restaurant, having just been slugged from behind by a character named Eddie "Punchy" McLaughlin. Punchy, a Charlestown loan shark, had tried to break Tommy's skull with something heavy wrapped in a folded newspaper.

On the Boston waterfront, where both Sullivan and McLaughlin were known, Sullivan was a local hero, a standup guy who didn't like bullies, a good Catholic boy who still lived at home with his mother. He was also a former boxer, a light-heavyweight who had lost only twice in twenty-two professional bouts. Now, though, Sullivan was down on the floor, his scalp laid open. Satisfied that his job was done, Punchy strutted out of the place. What he hadn't counted on was Sullivan's recuperative powers. Though his blood was pouring onto the restaurant's floor, Sullivan began to stir. As if an imaginary referee were counting over him, he rose to his feet. He steadied himself.

Then he went out onto Boylston Street, found Punchy, and proceeded to beat the fuck out of him.

It's fun to imagine how Punchy reacted when he saw Tommy coming out of O'Keefe's. There was Tommy, blood on his face, walking toward him like an avenging Irish angel. Tommy had been out of the ring for a few years, but he was still an imposing figure with shoulders as wide as a doorway. The irony was that McLaughlin had been a boxer, too, but not a good one. And despite years of bopping people with lead pipes, he wasn't in any condition for a real fight.

According to local mythmakers, McLaughlin tried to save his ass by rolling under a parked car. With the incredible strength that had made him a hero among the local children, Sullivan allegedly lifted one end of the car and rested it on the curb. Then he reached under and dragged Punchy out for some more abuse. Legend has it that one of Tommy's punches tore off a piece of Punchy's ear, and a hook to the groin made Punchy scream so loudly that he was heard all across Back Bay. It just wasn't Punchy's night.

Why Punchy had attacked Tommy in the first place was a bit of a mystery. Chances are it stemmed from a disagreement on the docks, where Punchy was always causing trouble. In 1952, the year Sullivan knocked Punchy up and down Boylston Street, there were ongoing hostilities along Boston's waterfront. There'd been strikes, skirmishes, and an attempt by New York longshoremen to "gangsterize" the docks. Smelling money and opportunity, McLaughlin betrayed his local roots and sided with the New York men. The Boston dockworkers weren't having it. Long story short, Punchy attacked Sullivan and got his brains beaten out.

Sullivan had been a Boston favorite during the 1940s, fighting often at the Garden and the Boston Arena. Newspapers called him "The South Boston Strong Boy," which harkened back to the city's first boxing idol, John L. Sullivan. In fact, it was said that the nearly mythical John L. was a first cousin of Tommy's father.

The Boston press loved Sullivan's genial image and presented him in a variety of homespun poses: playing with his dog, reading bedtime stories to kids, showing neighborhood boys how to box. One Sunday

Globe headline read: "Tommy Sullivan, Southie's Newest Pride and Joy, Is Everybody's Pal." The *Globe*'s Jerry Nason once described Sullivan's personality this way: "There was no swagger to him, or any loud talk, and he was the sort of guy—even if you never in your life had watched him in a ring—you instinctively liked him."

Sullivan was a new kind of postwar boxing idol, a clean-cut fellow who didn't drink or smoke or mess around with women, but was built like a bulldozer, with fists that might've been formed at the nearby Quincy rock quarries. Best of all, his fair-haired image belied a pugnacious attitude; his fights were usually untamed brawls, which made him a favorite of Boston's hardcore boxing fans. A Tommy Sullivan bout always followed the same pattern: he'd spend the early rounds looking awkward and uncertain, but by the fourth he'd be hurling his overhand bombs. Opponents usually fell. Even rivals with concrete chins were turned to rubble.

Tommy was undefeated until he met crafty Cambridge middleweight Al "Red" Priest. In front of a nearly sold-out Garden crowd that, as one reporter claimed, "roared itself hoarse from start to finish," Tommy lost a majority decision to Priest in 1946. Though victorious, Priest was too weak to stand up in the shower after the bout. They clashed again in 1947. Sullivan fought hard—he even knocked Priest out of the ring in the seventh round—but once again, Priest won by decision. Tommy had a couple more fights but was increasingly bothered by fears that he might get hurt in the ring. He retired in 1949, his final bout being a ten-round decision win over Johnny Carter in Worcester. Sam Silverman, who often recalled the first Sullivan–Priest bout as the best fight between local men that he'd ever promoted, kept calling with offers. Sullivan wasn't interested.

He headed for the docks where he'd work for the next several years.

A few days before Christmas in 1957, Tommy Sullivan was murdered. It happened on East Fifth Street, the street he'd lived on since his birth. He'd just had dinner with his elderly mother and was on his way to work when somebody fired several shots at him. He was "found in a gutter about two hundred feet from his home," reported the United Press, "his head lying in a pool of blood." Police Lt. Joseph Doyle gave reporters the grim news that bullets had "nearly ripped off" Sullivan's face. Members of Sullivan's family had actually heard the sound of gunfire but thought it was coming from a movie they were watching on television.

A teenage girl had witnessed the shooting. She told police that four men in a dark sedan had driven up to Sullivan and called his name. When he turned, gunshots tore through the night. The girl noted the license plate began with "L21." Nine days later, a burned sedan answering the girl's description was found behind a coffee shop at the end of Hampshire Street in Cambridge. The police eventually ruled the car out—it was traced to a man in Somerville who worked for the airlines—and the case went cold.

It was believed that Sullivan had been gunned down by hired killers from New York in response to his part in the ongoing labor war among the longshoremen. Some thought he had been killed as an example to keep the other Boston dockworkers in line. Months later, police attempted to tie in Sullivan's murder with the slaying of John F. "Fats" Buccelli, head of a major narcotics ring that used the Boston docks as a drop-off location. Investigators believed the bullets found in Buccelli's head came from the same weapon used on Sullivan. It sounded promising, but nothing came of the investigation.

There were murmurs about Sullivan, though, murmurs that he was involved in criminal activity, that he wasn't so clean-cut after all, that he had started drinking and had strange friends. Most of it was just gossip. The truth is that no one knew much about Sullivan. A thirty-eight-year-old bachelor was bound to raise suspicion during those years when people were expected to marry young, but there wasn't much you could throw at Sullivan that would stick.

Years later, in a correspondence with a journalist interested in the case, James "Whitey" Bulger wrote from prison that the killing of Sullivan wasn't carried out by New Yorkers but by a local lunatic named James "Spike" O'Toole.

Hatchet-faced and jug-eared, with thick hair swept up in a 50s style pompadour, O'Toole was a rabid character allegedly responsible for more than a few murders. According to the O'Toole legend, when Boston crime figure Edward "Wimpy" Bennett decided he didn't want to pay off a debt to Roxbury loan shark Henry Reddington, he simply called O'Toole and said, "Reddington is screwing your girlfriend!" O'Toole burst into Reddington's office and blew him away, clearing Wimpy's debts in the process. Spike O'Toole was the kind of twitchy killer you see in old movies, bad tempered with a nervous trigger finger. It's not certain that Spike laughed maniacally when he killed a guy. Maybe he did.

He was also part of the McLaughlin crew of Charlestown.

Despite Bulger's claim that O'Toole murdered Sullivan, most sources say Sullivan's killing was orchestrated and carried out by Punchy McLaughlin. The math is as simple as a one-two to the head: Sully beats up Punchy; Sully ends up dead.

Though his name no longer registers with anyone but Boston's most ardent fight fans or crime buffs, or people old enough to have been his neighbor, there is a romantic mythology around Tommy Sullivan. When people hear his story, they draw comparisons to Terry Malloy, the character played by Marlon Brando in *On the Waterfront*. Like Sullivan, Malloy was an ex-boxer turned dockworker at odds with some dangerous men. But Malloy had it easy. Malloy never had someone like Punchy gunning for him.

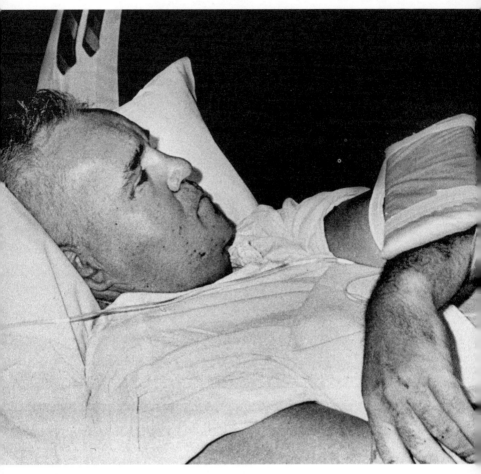

Eddie "Punchy" McLaughlin on his way to the hospital after the McLean gang's second attempt on his life. *AP Photo*

Eddie McLaughlin:
They Called Him "Punchy"

*The Best Killers in Boston Needed Three Tries
to Knock Him Off . . .*

As he reached middle age, you wouldn't think he was an ex-fighter, not with his bulbous head and his pear-shaped body. Of course, his flattened nose was an obvious tip to his pugilistic past, but to most he looked like a sleepy-eyed drunk, gray-haired and gone to fat. Yet, when Edward J. McLaughlin was young, he fought in both amateur and professional rings, and at one time was considered a good local prospect. He'd been a Charlestown kid, one of ten children born to railroad clerk John McLaughlin and his Irish-born wife, Annie. He'd grown up in one of those cramped, unfriendly districts where fighting was essential. He'd also been a bold thief with a taste for shoplifting, but fighting was in his head and his heart. He went from doing it in the street to doing it in the ring, winning some acclaim in local amateur tournaments.

In 1935, the amateur career of Eddie McLaughlin came to a climax when he competed for the prestigious New England Diamond Belt, a major event drawing the best amateur boxers from all six New England states. A photograph of a teen McLaughlin was used in advertisements for the show. He's not the bloated forty-year-old the city would someday know and fear; he's slim, with short arms and coltish legs and a none-too-bright expression. He lost in the semifinal to Lowell's Eddie Carroll.

In the professional ranks there was an "Eddie McLaughlin" who fought as a middleweight and listed himself as being from various places, including Cambridge and Charlestown. He competed sporadically during the late 30s and early 40s, and even fought, and lost by TKO, to the same Eddie Carroll of Lowell. In his final recorded bout, he notched a points win over Ted Lowry, a capable journeyman who would one day give Rocky Marciano a pair of tough fights. Lowry thumped Eddie to the canvas in the final round, but Eddie beat the count and survived to the bell. It had been a close call, perhaps enough to convince him to take up a life of crime. The general sense of this McLaughlin as a fighter was that he wasn't bad, but he couldn't take a punch.

There was also an "Eddie McLaughlin" of Boston who fought in North Adams around the same time, losing twice to a North Adams middleweight named Fiere Maruco (alias "Young Carnera") in 1936–1937. These two Eddie McLaughlins were more than likely the same fighter, the future loan shark and murderer. He picked up the nickname "Punchy," though no one in his family referred to him that way. In 1947, a fight card in Skowhegan, Maine, featured the debut of "Bernard McLaughlin." This was probably Punchy's brother Bernie. If so, Bernie lost his one and only pro bout to a fellow from Waterville known as "Young Champagne."

By the 1950s, Punchy, Bernie, and youngest brother Georgie had become notorious in Boston's underworld. They made their names as enforcers for North End underboss Jerry Angiulo and ran their own loan-sharking business on the waterfront. They'd help you get work, but if you didn't kick back part of your pay, the McLaughlins were quick to bust heads. Their favored weapon: a lead sash weight wrapped in newspaper.

Punchy was the eldest McLaughlin, and the muscle of the group; in 1951, he allegedly led a raid in South Boston, rousting and pistol-whipping longshoremen who had refused to cross a picket line. When local men rallied to combat Punchy's goon squad, he purportedly fired a gun in the air and fled the scene, his team of thugs following. It was all in a day's work for a guy whose job was listed on his police record as "union delegate."

With the addition of Charlestown gunmen Stephen and Connie Hughes, the McLaughlins grew more dangerous. Punchy, though, was the most notorious of the brothers. "He could shoot you and smile," said one associate. He never lost his flair for shoplifting, even when he was grown. One time he was caught boosting a pink negligée. Why he wanted it was never clear, but he was held for extra questioning by police who thought he might be the Boston Strangler. He wasn't. Punchy was many things, but not a killer of women.

At a Labor Day party on Salisbury Beach in 1961, Punchy's younger brother Georgie behaved inappropriately with the girlfriend of another man, a character known as "Bobo" Petricone. Under most circumstances, this would've been just another case of Georgie acting like a jerk. But on this particular weekend, he was in the company of two toughs from Somerville's Winter Hill Gang. Not appreciating Georgie's rude behavior, they promptly gave him the beating of the decade.

After they dumped Georgie on the front lawn of a nearby hospital, they described the incident to the leader of their gang, James J. "Buddy" McLean. Buddy told them to forget about it. Buddy still listed himself as a longshoreman or truck driver, but he was Boston's Irish crime boss, a Somerville figure of legendary status, a man so mean that he once gained information by putting a blow torch to a rival's genitals. He didn't feel there was much to worry about.

Georgie survived the walloping from Winter Hill, but when Punchy and Bernie realized McLean had no intention of punishing his two flunkies for what they'd done, the McLaughlins vowed revenge.

Punchy had a long rivalry with McLean. It's been said that the McLaughlins had once tried to enlist him as a skull-cracker, an offer he refused. In 1960, when McLean was readying to box a Charlestown brawler named Butchie Quinn, Punchy and his crew showed up at the outdoor venue packing heat. With a $2,000 bet riding on the Charlestown fighter, the McLaughlins loudly hinted that a McLean victory would land him in the morgue. McLean destroyed Quinn in less than a round, and with his own growing entourage of psychopaths around him, stared the McLaughlins down as he made his way out of the ring. "You owe me two grand," he said to Punchy. This, of course, was a playful romp compared to what would happen as a result of the Labor Day party gone awry.

The ensuing years saw a vicious, ever-escalating street battle known alternately as "The McLean–McLaughlin War," "The Charlestown–Winter Hill War," or "The Boston Irish Gang War." That the rival gangs were headed by former amateur boxers was usually lost in the newspaper coverage, which was understandable since the battle would be highlighted by daytime shootouts, car bombs, assassinations, and even a beheading. This raging street war was longer and bloodier than most New York Mob wars. Depending on the source, the casualty count was between forty and seventy. At one point, depressed over the number of dead bodies strewn across the city, Punchy allegedly remarked, "All of this over a broad."

McLean decided in 1964 that Punchy had to be killed. McLean had knocked off Bernie McLaughlin a couple years earlier, shooting him during the lunchtime rush in Charlestown's City Square. McLean and Petricone were arrested and questioned in connection to the murder of Bernie, but were released. (Petricone's gangster career was short-lived. He soon left for California, took acting lessons, changed his name to "Alex Rocco," and made a career of playing slime balls and tough guys, including attorney Moe Greene in *The Godfather* and Jimmy Scalise in the classic Boston crime flick *The Friends of Eddie Coyle*. During the making of the latter, he allegedly introduced star Robert Mitchum to members of the Winter Hill Gang.)

Since McLean had attracted some heat with the killing of Bernie, he decided the best way to whack Punchy was to enlist outside help. He recruited a team of cold-blooded local killers: Joe Barboza, Stephen

Flemmi, and Frank Salemme. The ruthless trio was among the best in the killing business, but they'd never find a more difficult and resilient target than Punchy.

The gunmen—and it has never been certain which of them were involved—made their first attempt on Punchy in November of 1964. Dressed as rabbis, they approached Punchy in a Brookline parking lot and opened fire into his new Oldsmobile. They didn't kill him, but they did manage to blow off part of his jaw. Covered in blood, Punchy staggered toward the nearby Hotel Beaconsfield and asked for help. Then he went outside and collapsed on the sidewalk in front of a barbershop. Punchy found himself at Beth Israel Hospital where his face was put back together with metal pins.

Punchy, of course, hadn't survived for so long in Boston's underworld without having the wiles of an alley cat. One afternoon, months after that first attempt on his life, he was certain that a pair of Winter Hill men were following him. He ducked into a Brockton department store and purposely let himself get caught shoplifting. Surrounded by store security and police, he felt safe. It was, however, a Pyrrhic victory. His brother Bernie had already been killed, and Georgie was soon to be tried for murder. Punchy's wife had left him and wanted a divorce. And though he'd escaped trouble this time, there was more to come.

The next attack on Punchy came in the summer of 1965. This time the shooters blew off his right hand. He managed to drive himself to a nearby gas station where he asked for help before passing out.

From the hospital bed where he'd been fitted with a prosthetic hand, Punchy treated the newspapers to a round of poor-pitiful-me. He claimed to know nothing about any gang war, and didn't understand why anyone wanted him dead; he worried that someone near him might get hit by accident. Gunmen, he said, were usually high on pills and didn't care if innocent people were hurt. He also wanted to remind people that not all the McLaughlins were bad, and that he had two older brothers who had been killed during World War II. Punchy's plea for understanding must've sounded to reporters like a Charlestown aria, performed by a jawless, one-handed mug whose time was running out.

What Punchy didn't know was that Barboza, Flemmi, and Salemme had a new accomplice, FBI agent Paul Rico. It was alleged that Rico had a special hatred for Punchy because the McLaughlins had threatened to blackmail him over his alleged dalliance with some underage boys. Rico, who mingled comfortably with the worst of Boston's underworld, found out where Punchy was staying and gave the address to the killers. According to FBI records, Rico had already turned Buddy McLean into an informant. Helping Buddy's crew track down Punchy was an early example of the FBI's willingness to work with criminals in order to get information.

The end for Punchy came on October 20, 1965. He was boarding a bus in West Roxbury on the way to Georgie's trial when a wigged gunman fired on him. Punchy tried to run but stumbled and fell. He'd been holding a paper bag with a gun in it, but before he fell he handed it off to a random woman and told her to get rid of it. He knew if he lived he'd be in trouble for possessing a weapon; even as he was being shot at, the wheels in his head were turning. (Why he was bringing a gun to his brother's trial is a question that remains unanswered, though it may have been for protection.)

As Punchy lay on the pavement, the killer took careful aim and shot him several times. According to Boston's Mob folklore, the killer purportedly put an exclamation mark on his work by taking careful aim and shooting Punchy in the balls. Barboza would take credit for killing Punchy, but most other sources say Flemmi or Salemme did the shooting. Salemme testified before Congress in 2003 that he had participated in most of the killings of the McLaughlin gang, "planned them and did them."

Punchy was taken to Faulkner Hospital in Dorchester where he died. The coroner noted there were bullets in his heart, lungs, spleen, liver, and intestines. As the doctors tore open his blood-soaked shirt to work on him, they might've been able to make out the tattoos on his chest—an

36

American flag, an eagle, a ship, a girl. Of course, with his torso torn apart by bullets, the artwork may not have been visible. Brother George, whose goofy behavior had kicked off the entire McLean–McLaughlin war, heard the news of Punchy's murder while he was at Suffolk Superior Court. "That's the ballgame," he said.

Punchy was buried at Holy Cross Cemetery in Malden, not far from the resting place of Sparky Chiampa. His slaughter had been a horror show for the people at the bus stop. If they'd been reading the newspaper coverage of the gang war, they might've known what was going on, but it's doubtful they recognized the murdered man as Eddie McLaughlin. They only saw a gray-haired man bleeding to death, not knowing that he'd once been a pitiless loan shark who had terrorized the waterfront, or that he'd once been a contender for the New England Diamond Belt.

Joe Barboza was a proud rat. *Bettman Archive/ Getty Images*

Joe Barboza:
The King of East Boston

*Boston's Most Sadistic Killer Dreamed of
Boxing Glory . . .*

People who knew Joe Barboza say he had a scary presence about him, a mix of remorselessness and rage that undoubtedly served him well during his years as Boston's most brutal underworld killer. Even when he was dressed in one of his favorite mohair suits, something about Barboza reminded one of a Neanderthal who might attack you with a club or a rock. Even the most vicious of Boston's mobsters didn't want him around.

Among his less desirable attributes was his habit of biting people. He bit so many of his enemies that it is easy to imagine him loping around the city's foggy streets like a werewolf with blood dripping from his fangs. The most famous bite of his career took place at the Ebb Tide lounge in Revere. One night Henry Tameleo, an older member of the New England Mob, saw Barboza smack somebody a little too hard. Tameleo told Barboza to stop using his hands on people. Barboza promptly leaned forward and sank his teeth into his rival's ear. As the victim howled in pain, Barboza looked at Tameleo.

"See that?" Barboza said. "I didn't use my hands."

That was allegedly the night Barboza was dubbed "The Animal."

Boston crime buffs have made Barboza into a sort of cult figure, but there hasn't been much written about his boxing career. The sport meant enough to him that he had an image of boxing gloves tattooed on his left arm. Tattooed on the right arm: *Born to Lose*.

Barboza allegedly began boxing in the early 1950s while serving time in prison for burglary. Barboza's father had boxed a bit. Joe had hated his old man and seemed determined to surpass him in the boxing trade. When he wasn't getting high on paint thinner or rumbling with the guards at MCI-Norfolk, Barboza focused on the ring.

Barboza wasn't precisely built for the sport, his peculiar body seemingly assembled by drunken pranksters. An enormous torso topped off his stubby legs, which wasn't exactly a blueprint for mobility. His head, a masterpiece of nature gone askew, was oversized. His massive chin was as inviting to hit as the left field wall at Fenway Park. He was tough, though. Bobby Quinn, at one time a promising heavyweight, sparred a bit with Barboza when both were incarcerated. Quinn said you could beat on Barboza until your hands ached.

Barboza ended up at the Concord Reformatory, where prison psychiatrists decided he was much smarter than he looked. (He once talked a guard into helping him smuggle knives into the prison that he would sell to other inmates.) Ultimately, Barboza was diagnosed as a sociopath beyond rehabilitation. Yet this killer of numerous men was able to talk a woman into marrying him, which has to qualify as a certain kind of charm.

Though his prison adventures included organizing an escape with some other inmates and nearly beating a guard to death with a wooden table leg, he somehow managed an early release in 1958. By then, he'd made up his mind to pursue two dreams. The first was to become a professional boxer. The second was to be the first non-Sicilian to become a fully made member of the Mafia.

As a Portuguese thug from New Bedford, there was no chance Barboza would be accepted into La Cosa Nostra. Granted, Boston's new crop of

young Italian men was less interested in the Mob than previous genera-
tions had been, which meant non-Italians were often recruited for dirtier
assignments, opening doors for a loon like Barboza. But as far as being a
made man, Barboza was lost in a fantasy. Then again, this was a man who
sometimes signed letters as "The King of East Boston."

As for boxing, he approached boxing trainer/manager Johnny Dunn
of Chelsea and asked for help. Dunn, who would later work with such
famous names as Bob Foster and Micky Ward, quickly had Barboza
fighting in North Adams and Fall River. He won two out of three bouts
before he was busted for burglary and sent to Walpole State Prison. He
still had boxing on his mind when he was paroled in 1960. This time,
Barboza planned to do some loan-sharking on the side to pay for his
training expenses. He also made himself available as a sparring partner
at the New Garden Gym on Friend Street. It was there that Barboza met
Joe DeNucci.

"I was contacted about this guy who just got out of the can and wanted
some work as a sparring partner," DeNucci said. "He was strong, but he
didn't know what he was doing. I'd just play with him, jab him, and he'd
curse at me."

Barboza's volcanic temper could come to the surface in only a second.
It was as if he had two modes: vaguely calm and inferno.

"Johnny Dunn owned a store that sold motor scooters, and Joe worked
there part-time," DeNucci said. "He asked me to make sure Joe got to
work on time, because he needed to stay out of trouble. One afternoon
we're stuck in traffic. A truck driver in front of us thought we were too
close, so he gave us the finger. Joe says, 'Do you have anything sharp?'
He reaches into my glove compartment and finds a little penknife, the
kind you'd use to slice an orange. He takes that tiny knife and he gets out
of the car. The truck's window was open so Joe just reaches in and starts
stabbing the truck driver. He must've stabbed that guy twenty times in
the arm. I think the driver was in shock; he couldn't believe what was
happening. Can you imagine all those little stab wounds? You couldn't

do much damage with that small knife, but Joe tried. Then he got back in my car and acted like nothing happened."

If this incident didn't convince DeNucci that Barboza was unstable, Barboza's behavior during a sparring session with Cardell Farmos certainly did. "Barboza thought Farmos was making a fool of him," said DeNucci. "Before you know it, Joe goes to his locker and comes back with a gun. He's yelling, 'You think you're gonna show me up?' He starts shooting up the place. Three or four times he shot, into the ceiling, everywhere. Fighters and trainers are running for cover, hiding anywhere they can, diving under the ring, hiding behind heavy bags."

Despite his uncontrolled temper, Barboza won six of his next seven fights and was featured in a major boxing magazine as "Prospect of the Month." He had changed the spelling of his name to "Barbosa" and was lying about his record, claiming he was 10-0, bragging to the *Globe* that he would be a leading contender in just a few months' time. But then it all came tumbling down. In September of 1961, he fought a journeyman named Don Bale at the Garden. An Idaho middleweight coming off two straight losses, Bale should've been an easy night for Barboza. Instead, Bale landed a shot on Barboza's colossal chin and knocked him out in the sixth.

Perhaps the loss to Bale made him realize he'd never be of championship caliber. Or maybe the call of the streets was just too tempting. Whatever the reason, Barboza quit the ring at age twenty-nine, leaving a record of 8-3 with five knockouts.

"Joe was tough, but he didn't have much ability," said fellow New Bedford fighter Jimmy Connors. "He had a pretty good right hand, and he came to fight, but he was more interested in hanging around with the wrong people. Poor Joe. God bless him."

Boxing's loss was a gain for Boston's underworld. In a short time, Barboza was known as the most brutal hired killer in the city. At one time it was believed that his reign of terror included the murder of twenty-six people, though that number has dropped a bit over time and is impossible to verify. What he believed was that the Mafia would have to induct him if he piled up enough bodies.

Barboza was an equal opportunity killer, making himself available to the North End Mob, the Patriarca faction out of Providence, and Buddy McLean's gang in Somerville. Barboza and McLean had a link beyond a mutual interest in boxing in that McLean had been adopted by Portuguese parents and had married a Portuguese woman. Perhaps taking a cue from McLean, Barboza also organized his own crew of miscreants, a kind of East Boston wolf pack. When he wasn't involved in contract killings, Barboza made quick money by intimidating people who were causing trouble for his friends. A favorite method of his was to follow you into a darkened movie theater and beat you senseless.

Other times he'd visit you at your place of business, usually accompanied by his right-hand man, Ronald "Ronnie the Pig" Cassesso, a former North Ender who bore a resemblance to Al Capone, had Capone been blown up into a Macy's parade float. (Cassesso is not to be confused with another Boston gunman, "Vinnie the Pig" DeVincent, or Alfredo "The Blind Pig" Rossi, a Providence fence who sold mink jackets out of his basement.) With their upturned coat collars, felt hats, and dark glasses, Barboza and Ronnie the Pig were a pair of hulking thugs from your nightmares. North End businessmen must've been terrified at the sight of them.

Little did Barboza's crew know that "The Animal" would soon be collaborating with FBI agents. Years prior to Whitey Bulger doing it, Barboza flipped and became an informant. He felt the Mafia had disrespected him. He'd learned what others had learned: the Mob didn't hold ex-fighters in particularly high esteem. The breaking point may have been when he was in jail on gun charges, and two of members of his East Boston crew were killed and robbed of his bail money by members of the New England Mob.

Barboza cozied up to the FBI quickly. For his protection, the most famous rat since Joe Valachi was held at Thatcher Island off the coast of

SLAUGHTER IN THE STREETS

Rockport. To the puzzlement of his guards, Barboza spent much of his free time writing poetry and drawing pictures. "I had a love-hate feeling for the guy," said John Partington, the U.S. Marshall who had helped start the program where federal witnesses were given new identities. "He was a killer, but still, we had gotten close." Sometimes Barboza carped about the island. It was full of snakes. The feds treated him well, though. When Barboza complained of boredom, they set him up with a boxing gym so he could spar with the guards.

In the next few years, Barboza fingered several key members of the New England Mob for murder. Oddly, many of the people he named were innocent, and Barboza's reasons for helping frame them were never known. He even ratted on Ronnie the Pig, sending his old buddy to Walpole State Prison. The Pig whiled away the hours by managing the prison's gift shop.

For his help, Barboza served only one year in prison and was then sent to California as part of the FBI's new United States Federal Witness Protection Program. He played along for a while, but in 1971 he was involved in another caper and pleaded guilty to second-degree murder. Another prison stint followed, this time at Folsom. By now there was a price on his head, rumored to be a quarter of a million dollars.

In 1972, Barboza made his most bizarre public appearance, serving as a witness for the House Select Committee on Crime's investigation into Patriarca. Surrounded by fifteen guards armed with machine guns, Barboza took the stand and calmly announced that none other than Frank Sinatra was pals with Patriarca and had known of the New England Mob's efforts to fix horse races. Roused out of retirement to respond, Sinatra denied any involvement and called Barboza a "bum." The Committee's verdict was that Sinatra had been "an unwitting front," which was a mild victory for Barboza in his vendetta against Italians.

Barboza also teamed up with crime author Hank Messick to write a memoir, *Barboza*, which was full of lies and self-serving propaganda. Depicting himself as an almost heroic figure who wouldn't bend to the

Mob's demands, Barboza imagined the book would be made into a movie. Within months of its release, however, Barboza met his bloody end in San Francisco.

On February 11, 1976, a hired gunman from New England shot Barboza in a parking lot. The Animal died at the age of forty-two. Barboza's attorney, F. Lee Bailey, was succinct. "With all due respect for my former client," Bailey said, "I don't think society has suffered a great loss."

Barboza was found slumped against his car, blood flowing out of his side. Barboza's movie dream was dead, as was the dream of being the first Portuguese member of the Mafia. The dream where he became a boxing champion was dead, too, though that one had been dead a long time.

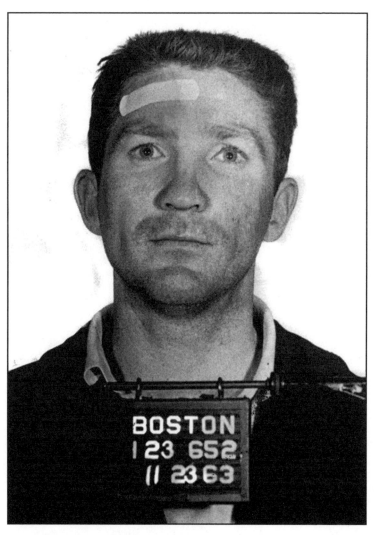

Two different killers took credit for Tony Veranis's
murder.

Tony Veranis:
The Tough Guy

*Boxing Was Good to Him; the Streets
Were Not . . .*

Tony Veranis was supposed to be one of the uplifting stories that come out of boxing, a Rocky Graziano type, a tough guy from the streets who had been in and out of correctional institutions since he was twelve. Boxing had saved him, he said. Boxing had straightened him out.

But stories can take unexpected twists.

When Veranis stepped into the ring to face Joe Devlin as part of Sam Silverman's St. Patrick's Day show at the Garden in 1958, he feared something might go wrong. True, Veranis could punch hard enough to shake the walls of the arena, but he didn't feel well. And it wasn't because he was fighting an Irishman on an Irish holiday. The problem was that he'd been getting headaches since his last fight. Bad ones. He didn't tell anyone. He was a tough guy. He'd fight through it. Sure enough, the bout with Devlin was a disaster. Devlin knocked him down several times before the bout was finally stopped at the end of the third. "I got hit so many punches I thought I was fighting the crowd," Veranis said. His record was now 26-2-2, much of it achieved in one year of breakneck activity. Silverman told him to rest; a young firebrand like Veranis could be recycled, even after a devastating loss.

Four weeks later, Veranis was at his Newton home when he collapsed. He was rushed to City Hospital where doctors spent three hours removing blood clots from his brain. A Catholic priest hovered over the scene, giving Veranis the last rites. Tony survived the operation but never fought again.

Born June 15, 1938, Tony Veranis was the son of Italian immigrants living in Dorchester. His parents occasionally brought Tony to the boxing matches at the old Mechanics Building on Huntington Avenue. Little Tony was mesmerized by the sight of local journeymen trading punches. It wasn't long before Tony was imitating his ring heroes in the street, using his fists against the neighborhood punks. He also succumbed to America's latest scourge: juvenile delinquency.

Veranis's bad behavior landed him a seat at the Lyman School for Boys, an ominous reform school outside the city. Other Lyman alumni included Punchy McLaughlin, Joe Barboza, and Albert DeSalvo (a.k.a The Boston Strangler).

While at Lyman, Veranis took part in boxing matches. He caught the attention of veteran fight manager Clem Crowley, who guided Veranis through a decent amateur career. By 1957, Veranis was ready to turn professional. "Boxing got me out of trouble," he said. "It does that for a lot of kids."

All was well for the former street hood as he won fight after fight. He was engaged to be married, he had the attention of Sam Silverman, and had a sporting-goods store footing the bill for his training expenses. He fought all over the New England circuit, thrilling spectators with his dynamic style and his powerful right lead. He was "right-hand crazy," forgetting all about his left and gambling everything on his right. He looked crude, but he stopped fourteen of his opponents before the final bell. Bobby Murphy, who had been named boxing's Rookie of the Year in 1955 by Boston sportswriters, was knocked out in seven by Veranis and immediately retired. Rocky Ford, brought in from New York to fight Veranis, ended up in Mass General with a broken jaw. Crowley felt his young tiger was ready for anybody, even Tony DeMarco.

Veranis wasn't without quirks. When he earned a casual decision win over Gunboat Steeves, he seemed to be loafing. It turned out Tony didn't want to hurt him because Steeves had given him a ride to the arena. On another occasion, Veranis canceled a bout because he'd eaten some strawberries that gave him hives. But even these stories added to the growing legend of Tony Veranis, the teen terror, the reform-school kid with a mule-kick punch.

Then came the headaches. He spent his twentieth birthday recovering from brain surgery. He told reporters that he wasn't too upset that his career was over, but he praised the business, even if it had nearly killed him. "Boxing was good to me," he said. "I met a lot of good and honest people of all classes. A lot of people call boxing a dirty racket. But to me it was clean all the way."

Now, though, he faced an uncertain future. The wedding was off. There were mounting medical bills. He had no job. He said he might stay around boxing as a trainer or work with kids.

"I'd start fighting again if I could," he said. "It's much better than getting kicked in the street or ending up in jail."

He ended up in jail.

In 1960, Veranis robbed a cab driver of twenty-two dollars. This earned him a three-year stay at MCI-Norfolk. Upon his release, Veranis drifted. He started drinking and feeling sorry for himself. He worked construction jobs. He splurged on gifts for his parents when he had a few bucks in his pocket, but he was clearly struggling. "He was a good kid," said the *Globe*'s Bud Collins, "as nice as I've met in sports. Confused, I guess, but trying to find the right way."

On April 26, 1966, the body of Tony Veranis was found at the bottom of an embankment in the Blue Hills section of Quincy. Veranis had been pistol-whipped and had bruises on his body. It appeared as if someone had spent a half hour kicking him. He'd also been shot in the head. The medical examiner described it as "a real professional job." The tough guy was dead at age twenty-eight.

The popular story is that Veranis made the mistake of crossing John Martorano, an associate of Whitey Bulger known as "The Basin Street Butcher." Martorano and his brother Jimmy were loan sharks, and Veranis supposedly owed them money. When Jimmy approached Veranis in what Martorano described as a "Southie bar," Veranis gave him a smack and sent him on his way. When Martorano heard this, he tracked Veranis down in a Roxbury bar. This tale, told in 1995 by Martorano to Federal Prosecutor Fred Wyshak, sounded fanciful. Veranis allegedly pulled a gun on Martorano and then, in self-defense, Martorano pulled his own weapon and shot Veranis in front of "thirty or forty" witnesses. Not only did Martorano expect people to believe this "gunfight at the OK Corral" scenario, he also described Veranis as being surrounded by women, acting abrasive, and telling Martorano to go fuck himself. Granted, it's possible that Veranis was drunk and obnoxious, but the story doesn't account for Veranis looking like he'd been severely beaten before anyone shot him. In 1999, Martorano confessed to several killings to cut a deal with investigators. Veranis was on the list, though Martorano was never charged with his murder.

Martorano gave a slightly different version of the story years later to author Howie Carr. This time, instead of his brother Jimmy getting slapped by Veranis, it was Tommy DePrisco, a member of Joe Barboza's crew. Martorano also changed the location of the shooting from Roxbury to Dorchester.

Martorano's inconsistent storytelling leads some to doubt him. It's more likely that Martorano and someone else—these killers rarely worked alone—took Veranis aside and worked him over before killing him. The medical examiner had noted the angle of bullet entry. It appeared Veranis had been shot in the head while on his knees. Perhaps he'd spent his final moments begging for his life.

The most glaring problem with Martorano's tale is that someone else had confessed to killing Veranis many years earlier.

William Geraway, a hoodlum with a history of violent crime, robbery, and forgery, supposedly killed Veranis because the two had gotten into an argument and Veranis slugged him. Later, Geraway told Veranis that he knew of a safe on Castle Island that could be burgled and invited Veranis to help. Geraway's scenario depicts a pitiful Veranis, punch-drunk and slow-witted, happily getting into Geraway's car to be driven to his doom in Quincy. Geraway supposedly overpowered him, beat him up, and shot him. Geraway was so pleased with himself that he couldn't keep quiet. One night he made a drunken confession to another creep who, in turn, squealed to Boston detective Joe McCain.

Taking the tip seriously, McCain began snooping around Castle Island. He found a young woman who had been there the night of the murder. She'd seen two men fitting the description of Veranis and Geraway. She later identified photographs of Veranis and Geraway at the district attorney's office and testified before a grand jury. In a bizarre turn, Geraway was acquitted of murdering Veranis but was found guilty of killing a young man named David Sidlauskas, a friend of Veranis whose body was also dumped in Quincy. Geraway, already serving a sentence for counterfeiting, received a life sentence at Walpole State Prison.

Geraway would later rat out Joe Barboza for a murder, be released from prison, and go on to become a kind of minor celebrity. He went on the lecture circuit to speak on various topics, including the death penalty, the Mafia, and prison reform. He even authored a book about his felonious life.

With the story of Veranis, a lot that was loathsome and depressing about boxing and Boston's underworld came to light. Perhaps the longest lasting part of his legend was the tattoo on the fingers of one hand that spelled "Luck." You needed some to survive in his circle. His ran out long before his body was found in Quincy.

MURDER VICTIM: Rocco DISEGLIO, alias Rocco DESIGLIO, Rocco DISEGLEO, Rocco DISIGLIO,
                Rocco SEGLIO, "Rocky" DISIOLIO, MBI 183014, FBI 612548C,
                Middx. Co. HC 139187, Billerica HC 26730, PD Watertown 2007

GIST: Body found in car parked in wooded section off Rowley Bridge St., Topsfield
       on 6-16-66 by State Trooper after tip by Boston Police. Bullet hole in back
       of subject's head. Victim's car was Thunderbird Sedan, Mass. Reg. R34-822.

INVESTIGATING DEPARTMENTS: Topsfield PD and Mass. State Police

DESCRIPTION: Born 4-11-39 in Italy, MW, 5'7½", 147 lbs., dark brown hair, brown eyes,
              med. build, dark comp., parents, Salvatore & Concetta (DeSantis),
              wife, Joanne; Tattoos: "Rocco" & woman on right arm, playing card spade
              on back of left hand, "X" on left hand; scar on left wrist.

ADDRESSES: West St., Newton (at death)   364 Watertown St., Newton
                145 Riverview Ave., Waltham   369 Watertown St., Newton
                17 Dalby St., Newton   52 Clyde St., Newtonville

OCCUPATIONS: Boxer, laborer

CRIMINAL RECORD: 1957 PD Newton, A & B, 6 mos. HC, 1957 E. Cambridge HC A & B 6 mos.,
                  1961 PD Watertown Poss. Burg. Tools & Att. B & E (nt), Prob. 6 yrs.
                  on each, 1962 Waltham Court Larc. under false pret., filed, 1962
                  Newton Court Gaming Pub. Place, filed, 1963 Middx. Sup. Crt. Larc. (7),
                  Larc. (3), Burg. Imp. in Poss., Prob. 2 yrs., Prob. 2 yrs., 5 yrs. 1 day
                  MCI Concord, susp. prob. 5-22-67, 1963 Middx. Sup. Crt. Att. B & E (nt),
                  prob. 5-22-67.

ASSOCIATES: Robert A. Ciolfi, MBI 218547   Joseph DeNucci, MBI 210875

ADDED INFORMATION:

Photo February 1961
FPC (Rt. middle reproduced)
U-19 U-18 U-6   U-19 U-12
W-I W-O U-14 U-16 U-11
MSBI BULL 4-65, Supp. 10-18-66

The police report filed after Rocco DiSeglio's
murder.

Rocco DiSeglio:
Gambling Man

He Liked Being a Criminal, but Not for Long . . .

On the morning of June 16, 1966, two Topsfield residents on their way to work noticed a burgundy Thunderbird parked in a wooded area just over the Danvers line. It looked abandoned. It looked suspicious. They notified the authorities. The night before, the East Boston police received an anonymous phone call from a male who said, "You can find a body in Danvers." Boston detectives enlisted the help of the Topsfield State Police, and it was State Trooper Warren W. Bailey who found the car. As he approached, he noticed the front windshield was shattered by bullet holes. Slumped in the passenger seat was a dead man who had been shot in the head. The detectives took special note of the victim's chic attire—bright yellow sports coat, black leather gloves, green pants—even though part of his face was gone and a bullet had torn out one of his eyes.

The body was taken to Hunt Memorial Hospital where it was identified as Rocco DiSeglio, a twenty-six-year-old ex-boxer from Newton. The police weren't sure if DiSeglio was part of the ongoing Boston gang war. He wasn't Irish, and he wasn't known to have criminal connections. He and his wife Joanne had one child; they lived a nondescript life well

SLAUGHTER IN THE STREETS

under the radar. Joanne told police that Rocco had been working construction jobs. He was found with more than $200 in his wallet, which ruled out robbery.

The murder scene had the earmarks of a gangland execution.

The police didn't know Rocco was a budding crook with a brazen attitude. He and a crew of three men had been robbing high-stakes dice games in the area. During a three-week stretch earlier in the year, they had robbed five different locations. These were Mob-run games, and Rocco was essentially robbing the Mob. There were rumors that a local mobster was running his own game and, angry that someone was stealing his business, had hired Rocco to set the competitors straight. Rocco was brash. He didn't even wear a mask to hide his identity. He'd just show up with his gang, a couple of them armed with shotguns, and tell the surprised victims that they shouldn't be running a game. The ex-welterweight was as daring as any robber anyone had seen in some time.

DiSeglio fought as "Rocky DiSiglio" from 1960 to 1964, putting up an underwhelming record of 4-4-1. He allegedly supplemented his meager boxing earnings by doing odd jobs for Raymond Patriarca. It was said that he once threw a fight so members of the Providence faction could make a few dollars by betting against him.

Eddie Grenke made his pro debut against DiSeglio at Memorial Stadium in Quincy on July 19, 1960. "Rocco was mainly a preliminary fighter," said Grenke. "No real style. I was scared shitless, because I didn't have a lot of experience, but he stayed away from me the whole fight. I thought I beat him, but they called it a draw. I think he was shown some favoritism because he was an Italian kid from Newton. He'd been Joe DeNucci's sparring partner, and DeNucci's people were very interested in him. He got what we used to call 'the Boston decision.'"

Born in Italy, DiSeglio didn't get to America until he was eight years old. Hampered by a language barrier, he quit school in the ninth grade and worked in a brother-in-law's construction company.

Crime came easily to him. He liked the rush of a robbery. There'd been occasions when his neighbors would leave their homes in the morning and see him sitting in his car. He looked as if he'd been up all night, buzzing from the adrenaline of the job. He'd be laughing to himself, wired. He'd call people over and tell them slightly veiled stories about his new life. Sometimes DiSeglio played with the details. Sometimes he said he wasn't the robber at all, but that he was just another of the players who had been robbed. Other times he'd say he was working for the Mob and that more games would be knocked off soon.

When Rocco held up these games, his method was to make his victims take off their pants. This way they couldn't follow him into the street. After the other robbers had gone through their wallets and taken their money, they would toss the pants into another room. Then Rocco and the boys would run out, leaving the dupes scrambling around to put their trousers back on. By the time they were dressed, DiSeglio and his crew were long gone. On one particular night, one of the players, a rotund Italian gambler from the old country, wasn't wearing any underwear. Not only did he suffer the indignity of being robbed, he had to stand there fully exposed for several minutes. Rocco liked telling this story. Unfortunately for him, he only got to tell it a few times.

DeNucci had known DiSeglio well; they were both Newton boys. He told the *Globe* about the fighter's out-of-control passion for gambling. "He had to have action all the time," DeNucci said.

It could be that DiSeglio's gambling background helped in his drift from boxing into crime. He was a risk taker. Boxers, gamblers, and criminals are all risk takers. To fight for a living, to put a lot of money down on a long shot, to rob someone at gunpoint, requires an element of risk unknown to the average person. For DiSeglio, robbery may have been a natural progression from boxing and gambling. To his way of thinking, it was better than working construction; he knew the risk and the risk was worth it. Right up until he was killed.

"I knew Rocco pretty well," DeNucci said years later. "He loved to gamble. A lot of us did. And the old-country Italians ran what they called 'barboot,' a dice game where a lot of money changed hands. Before there were things like scratch tickets and the weekly state lottery, people got deeply involved in these games. They were big all over the city.

"I never thought of him as a Mob guy. But he'd let you know that he had friends who might be connected. Maybe he was bragging a little, talking about his new buddies. He thought they were funny," said DeNucci.

The DiSeglio murder turned out to be a major newsmaker. The reason was the star witness: Joe Barboza.

The Animal, who had legally changed his name to "Joseph Baron," was now living under heavy supervision as an informant. He claimed to know exactly what had happened to Rocco DiSeglio. As Barboza told it, New England underboss Jerry Angiulo didn't like DiSeglio's reckless style and ordered him killed. Not only that but Angiulo gave the assignment to Rocco's own partners, Bernard Zinna, Mario Lepore, and Richard DeVincent (alias "Vinnie the Pig"). Barboza claimed to have heard this directly from Zinna and Vinnie the Pig, and to have seen the killers leaving together on the night DiSeglio was killed. The Animal also took credit for calling the East Boston police and telling them about the body in Danvers.

This was all good enough for prosecutors. The feds assembled a grand jury. In January of 1968, reporters flocked to Boston's Suffolk Superior Court to see if Barboza could help put away a few more Mafia types.

By this time the country was knee-deep in Mafia lore. The confessions of Joe Valachi in 1963 and the ongoing crackdown on organized crime had filled the public's imagination with Mob mythology. Hence, the murder of this unknown ex-welterweight became national news. People had been seeing Italian gangsters on television for years, and here was Angiulo, a living and breathing Italian mobster on trial for having ordered the death of an underling, an ex-fighter named "Rocco," no less. It was exciting stuff for the day.

As expected, Barboza provided plenty of drama in the courtroom. Under cross-examination by defense attorney Joseph J. Balliro, Barboza stiffened when he was accused of testifying only to help sell a memoir he was working on, a memoir that would see an increase in sales if his testimony resulted in more guilty verdicts. Barboza roared, "I'm up here telling the truth!" At one point DeVincent's attorney theorized that Barboza had actually killed DiSeglio. Barboza fired back that DeVincent was the killer and that Vinnie the Pig had grown egotistical and wanted to be a boss. According to the *Globe*, the prosecution's witness was "in a near rage" as he spoke.

Unfortunately, Barboza couldn't work his rat magic this time. Angiulo, Vinnie the Pig, Zinna, and Lepore were acquitted.

The reason, according to one of the jurors, was that Barboza didn't seem trustworthy.

The FBI eventually arrested Angiulo on racketeering charges in 1983, with help from those famous rats, Whitey Bulger and Stephen Flemmi. He spent more than twenty years in a federal prison.

According to Barboza's version of the story, Rocco DiSeglio was not really in charge of the robberies. He was simply the tip-off man, finding out where the games were being held and letting the real gunmen do the rest. Regardless of DiSeglio's exact role, no one was ever punished for his murder.

Then again, Zinna was whacked in 1969. Vinnie the Pig suffered the same fate in 1996.

Rico Sacramone heads to Somerville District Court after having shotgun pellets removed from his scalp. *The Boston Globe/Getty Images*

Rico Sacramone:
A Stylish Fighter

They Tortured Him Before They Killed Him . . .

During a January afternoon in 1973, a man in tattered clothes was seen walking along Route 495 in Lowell. He was talking to himself, dazed and bleeding. During those blitzed-out post-hippie years, a highway babbler wasn't such an unusual sight. Still, the police noticed a suspicious character was out there, a man who was possibly drunk or homeless and might get clobbered by traffic. When the man was brought in, he couldn't remember how he'd ended up on the highway or why his clothes were torn. All he knew was his name: Americo Sacramone.

He was taken to St. John's Hospital, where he gathered his thoughts. He told a weird tale about killing a man, a former friend named Joseph Brazil. Sacramone and Brazil had robbed a bank many years earlier; Brazil had been killed in 1971 in Charlestown. Now Sacramone claimed Brazil's friends had beaten him up and left him on the highway. Sacramone's story resulted in his being arraigned for murder in Charlestown District Court, but he was never brought to trial.

The police might have recognized his name if they'd been boxing fans. "Rico" Sacramone had been a highly regarded lightweight prospect who had fought three times at the Garden and once at the Boston Arena. As a teen fighting out of the blue-collar town of Everett, Sacramone had competed in local amateur tournaments; his bouts were often hailed as the most crowd-pleasing of the night. The *Globe* praised Sacramone in those days, describing him as a cagey kid, "whose boxing style is as old as the game itself."

With the looks of a movie star and a houseful of amateur boxing prizes, Sacramone seemed perfect for the Boston market. The Italian American boxing boom was near its end but still strong, and Sam Silverman and Rip Valenti were already on the lookout for another DeMarco. In March of 1957, as part of a Garden show headlined by DeMarco versus Larry Boardman, Sacramone made his pro debut along with another beginner, Joe DeNucci. Both were victorious, and at the time it was unknown which of the two would be Boston's next Italian American boxing star. It turned out to be DeNucci, who went on to have a long and respectable career, while Sacramone boxed for two years and quit with a record of 5-1.

If the police weren't aware of his ring career, they probably knew Rico for his affiliation with the Winter Hill Gang. He was allegedly Buddy McLean's bodyguard.

McLean's own boxing background is a subject of much speculation. He was said to have taken part in amateur bouts, but they were more of the unsanctioned summer carnival variety rather than anything remotely official. He had never considered turning pro, but he was known as a badass barroom brawler with more than one hundred knockout victims to his credit. According to the townie folklore, McLean trained daily as if preparing for a championship fight. Though he had the features of a choirboy, with a tiny pug nose and strawberry blond hair swept up like a 50s rocker, a closer look revealed the signs of a street brawler, namely a slightly damaged left eye and a face full of scars. There was even an incident where future middleweight champion Paul Pender ambled into a Somerville barroom with his entourage, supposedly looking for Joe Barboza. McLean, not liking Pender's attitude, chased the whole lot of them out into the street and beat up Pender's driver. Getting to the truth of McLean is difficult, though, since his biographers and admirers tend to imbue him with super strength and exaggerate his every move. His mystique was such that he left levelheaded people in a state of awe. "Buddy," said Jerry Forte, "would've killed Whitey Bulger with his bare hands."

The way McLean met Sacramone, not surprisingly, involved boxing.

After he quit the ring, Sacramone ended up at Norfolk for armed robbery. It was here that he first encountered McLean. Stories vary, but the gist is that the two former boxers engaged in a rough sparring session and, before an audience of cons howling like jackals, McLean left Sacramone unconscious with a broken jaw. That McLean was much bigger than Sacramone, and that prison guards would probably prevent a random gym session from going so far, means nothing to McLean's loyal mythmakers. But regardless of how the sparring played out, Sacramone and McLean became friends. McLean was released from Norfolk first; on the way out he invited Sacramone to look him up in the future.

Sacramone's link to McLean was solidified forever on October 30, 1965. On that night, McLean, Sacramone, and "Tony Blue" D'Agostino were in a Somerville bar. It was the Tap Royal on Broadway, Pal Joey's on Marshall Street, the Winter Hill Lounge, or the 318 Club, depending on which raconteur you want to believe. At closing time, the trio went out to where McLean's Buick Regal was parked, which happened to be next to the abandoned Capitol movie theater on Broadway. Hiding in the entrance of the boarded-up Capitol was a masked gunman from Charlestown, wielding a just-purchased pump-action shotgun from Sears. Out to avenge the recent murder of Punchy McLaughlin, the killer opened fire.

McLean died. Sacramone and D'Agostino survived.

Then again, survival is open to interpretation.

Sacramone came out of the hospital with his head wrapped in bandages. He looked like he was wearing a turban. The truth is that he was practically scalped by the gun blast and was lucky to be alive. Yet he'd been on parole the night McLean was killed, and being armed put Sacramone back in the can to finish his term for robbery.

When Sacramone was released, the Winter Hill hoods weren't exactly waiting with open arms. Some blamed him for McLean's murder. He'd allowed Charlestown to claim the top prize in Boston's longest and bloodiest street war.

Sacramone was never the same. Not only was his reputation sunk, he also grew increasingly paranoid. Brazil's friends were after him. McLean's gang wanted his head. Fearing a hired gunman might be standing around every corner, Rico became the epitome of the frazzled Mob lackey, a marginalized hood with no place to hide. Joe DeNucci was saddened at how the streets had broken his old friend.

"I saw him the night before he was killed," DeNucci said. "He was acting odd, like I was his enemy. It didn't make sense because we were close. I said, 'What's going on?' He didn't trust anybody at the time. I told him I wanted to talk to him, but I turned around and he was gone."

Many local boxers were coming to nasty ends during this period. There was Alfred "Indian Al" Angeli (real name: Alfred Notarangeli), a former amateur fighter who had muscled in on the Boston Mob's bookmaking business and was suspected of murdering a North End bookie. In April of 1974, Indian Al's body was found in the trunk of a car in Charlestown. John Martorano took credit for killing Angeli as a favor to the North End Mob.

An Angeli associate, James "Jake" Leary, was whacked in Florida just a year earlier. A good amateur featherweight from Medford, Leary was deeply involved in Angeli business. According to Martorano, it was one of the oldest and meanest of the Winter Hill killers, Joe McDonald, who had traveled to Fort Lauderdale and murdered Leary. The cold-blooded "Joe Mac" was a well-known underworld character. He had been Buddy McLean's friend and mentor and had even taught McLean how to box. McLean may have been dead, but there were still murderous maniacs out there, men like Joe Mac who would kill you for fun, which probably gave Sacramone reason enough to worry. If Joe Mac could find Leary in Florida, where the hell could Sacramone be safe?

Then there was Georgie Holden, a New England heavyweight. In August of 1973, Holden's body washed up on the banks of the Mystic River in Charlestown. He'd been shot in the head. That one went unsolved. There wasn't even much of an investigation.

Holden had been killed with a small-caliber handgun, which had become the Mob killer's weapon of choice. These little guns were lightweight, easy to conceal. Just step up to your man, put the gun behind his ear, and pop him. Sacramone undoubtedly knew the ways of hired killers. He probably knew that the tiny bullet entered the skull and zigzagged around the victim's brain, destroying it, cutting off the connection between the brain and the heart, and that the victim might not die immediately but would go into a kind of shock. The dying man's heart, in one last pump, would cause blood to squirt in a stream that could reach a length of two feet or more. Such images were probably haunting Sacramone as each day passed.

Sacramone's body was found February 2, 1975. He'd been shot in the temple and dumped in a swamp near the Saugus racetrack on Route 107, his shoeless feet bound together by wire. He was thirty-seven. Willie Fopiano, a small-time Boston thief, mentioned Sacramone in his 1993 memoir *The Godson*. He said, "Whoever whacked him tortured him first."

Rico Sacramone was just another Boston kid who fell in love with the cut-rate allure of gangsters. He paid for it. He paid first with his mind, then with his life.

Stevie Hughes (left) and Sammy Lindenbaum.
When they were killed, many considered the
McLean–McLaughlin war over. *Bettman Archive/
Getty Images*

Sammy Lindenbaum:
Boxer, Bandit, Abortionist

*Killed by a Gun Blast as He Drove, His Severed Fingers
Still Gripped the Steering Wheel . . .*

Had he been from New York instead of Boston, Sammy Lindenbaum would've been a cult figure. Though his Revere neighbors referred to him as a nice, quiet, old guy, he was in reality a cold-blooded character, with the reckless daring of a movie criminal. He got himself in such bizarre scrapes with the law that Damon Runyon or Jimmy Breslin would've turned him into an icon. When he was killed, shot by assailants while he drove down Route 114 in Middleton, bullets tore the fingers from his hand. According to the old stories, those fingers remained wrapped around the steering wheel and had to be pried off.

He never became a legend, though he certainly had the stuff from which legends are made. It could be that the exploits of this former flyweight boxer, which included robbing a grocery store while disguised as a woman, came at a time when newsrooms were busy with such twentieth-century icons as Babe Ruth, Jack Dempsey, and Charles Lindbergh. Or it could be that buttoned-up Boston didn't know how to exploit such a character, whereas any New York tabloid would've made Sammy a front-page sensation. Whatever the reason, Sammy Lindenbaum remains a forgotten figure in Boston crime annals, most likely because he was neither Italian nor Irish.

On September 23, 1966, Sammy was driving a rented Pontiac with Charlestown hood Stevie Hughes at his side. A black sedan pulled up alongside them. Then came a volley of armor-piercing bullets, tearing massive holes in the heads and chests of Lindenbaum and Hughes, killing them instantly. The car careened across three lanes and knocked down a hundred feet of guardrail before crashing into a swamp and landing on its side.

Hughes was the big news. Hughes was one of the last members of the McLaughlin gang. In fact, it had been Hughes who had killed Buddy McLean. With Hughes dead, there was speculation that the ongoing McLean–McLaughlin battle was coming to an end. This, more than Lindenbaum's death, was what grabbed news editors. That and the fact that Lindenbaum's two tiny dogs had survived and were cavorting in the weeds as police inspected the wreckage.

Lindenbaum (aka "Sammy Linden") was sixty-seven when he died. He was a short, pudgy man, but his dark, reptilian eyes held cruel secrets. He was known as a criminal whirlwind, with expertise in everything from illegal abortions to loan-sharking. He wasn't one to take lightly.

He was born in Russia in 1899, but as a child settled into Chelsea with his parents and five sisters. By age nineteen, he was boxing professionally in the Boston area using the alias "Young Leonard." In a 1920 census, he registered his occupation as "pugilist" and, with a Runyonesque touch, listed his industry as "fistic." He fought from 1918 to 1924, mostly in Massachusetts and New Hampshire. Record books list him at 10-20-4, which doesn't do justice to what appears to have been a crowd-pleasing style. "Fast and furious" was how a 1923 bout with Happy Harlan was described in the *Fitchburg Sentinel*. He was hired often to fight in the opening bout, meaning promoters knew he was a reliable performer who could get the show started.

But even as he found steady work in the ring, this 115-pound Russian immigrant couldn't stay out of trouble.

Lindenbaum's rap sheet went back to his teen years and included various busts for assault, burglary, fighting in public, and reckless driving. Apparently, he was also involved in a prostitution ring in Methuen. The ladies worked out of a tent on a hillside while Sammy, though his exact role was unclear, was probably responsible for luring horny men to the action. By 1922, he was involved with a married woman; the two bounced around from one shabby rooming house to the next in the Haverhill area. They had a volatile relationship—he was once seen threatening her with a gun, and they were also arrested and charged with "lewdness." "Linden has a long police record," reported the *Sentinel* in January 1925, "but seems to have the knack of keeping out of jail."

That newspapers had taken to calling him "Sammy Linden" brings up a curious side point. Around the time "Young Leonard" took a break in 1924, a 115-pound fighter named "Sammy Linden" of Chelsea appeared in upstate New York for a series of bouts. The *Syracuse Herald* described this Linden as an "experienced and clever performer who has fought all the leading midgets of New England." Oddly, Linden had no New England fights to his credit, but Young Leonard had been boxing there for years. Chances are, Sammy Linden and Young Leonard were the same man. There were quite a few fighters in the 1920s known as "Young Leonard" or "Kid Leonard," so it's likely that New York promoters didn't want another. Hence, Lindenbaum dumped the "Young Leonard" handle and was known for a few fights as "Sammy Linden." This could also explain how Lindenbaum was soon putting a gang together that included a New York couple, Frances Maffi and Bastino Roma. An eighteen-year-old girl from Lewiston, Maine, Blanch Dubois, finished the quartet; they were quickly in Lindenbaum's stomping grounds of Haverhill, robbing stores. This is when the "Bobbed-Hair Bandit" was born.

Accompanied by his three new partners in crime, Lindenbaum approached a Haverhill grocery store to rob it. The owner of the store, Walter Burnachie, claimed a small woman with bobbed hair and a purple mask barged in and stuck a pistol in his face. A man stood guard at the door while the masked female went through the cash drawer.

Just hours later, Lindenbaum and his gang were found hiding in a nearby house. A quick search by police revealed a pair of loaded revolvers, plus receipts from local pawnbrokers for a variety of watches and jewelry. The foursome was taken to the Haverhill station house for questioning. Burnachie pegged DuBois as the masked robber, but Lindenbaum stepped forward and said he, not the young woman, had committed the crime. He'd disguised himself as a female, he claimed, borrowing Dubois's clothes without her knowledge. The grocer said Lindenbaum looked like the man who had been at the door, but the Haverhill cops took Sammy's outrageous confession as gospel.

Newspapers across New England howled about the boxer turned cross-dressing bandit, describing in great detail how Lindenbaum had donned female clothes, a bobbed wig, and a purple mask to become, according to the *Sentinel*, "a stylish young woman."

Did Lindenbaum really dress as a woman, or was he simply trying to protect Dubois so she'd get a lighter sentence? He was certainly small enough to pass for a female. Besides, Lindenbaum liked waving guns around and brawling in the street; he wasn't likely to stand watch while some eighteen-year-old girl had all the fun. Apparently, the grocer never described the robber's voice, which might've cleared up the issue. Regardless, all four members of the Haverhill gang did some prison time for the robbery.

Sammy was out by 1930. Neither "Sammy Linden" nor "Young Leonard" fought during Lindenbaum's incarceration, but both appeared on a Portsmouth, New Hampshire, fight card months after Lindenbaum's release. Did Lindenbaum fight twice on the same night under two different names? Anything was possible during the Depression. Besides, a man who had dressed as a woman to rob a store wasn't above fighting twice the same night, especially if he was paid twice. (He lost twice, too. And he never fought again.)

After this failed attempt to restart his boxing career, Lindenbaum returned to crime. The next twenty years of his life was one act of larceny after another. He even reinvented himself as a backroom abortionist. For $450, he could make a pregnancy disappear. If something went wrong, he'd allegedly make the poor woman disappear, too. It's not clear where Sammy learned how to perform abortions, but Sammy knew a little about a lot. He didn't know how to stay out of jail, though. A widely publicized jewel heist in 1937 put him behind bars for more than a decade. During the 1950s, his activities included a bust for performing "illegal surgeries," an attempted murder of a New York lawyer, and burglarizing a cosmetics warehouse. So high was his criminal profile that he was even suspected of being part of the Brink's holdup; he wasn't. In 1959, Sammy led police on a high-speed chase through Lowell after robbing a grocery store of nearly $6,000. The wild pursuit ended when Sammy crashed his car into a building.

By the time Sammy got out of prison, he was in his sixties. The days of car chases and daredevil robberies were over for him; he invested in a laundry business and did some loan-sharking. What led to his doom, however, was his burgeoning friendship with the McLaughlins.

To befriend the McLaughlins during the 1960s was not smart. Yet Sammy was lending them money to rent cars and buy guns. This made him a marked man. Though Joe Barboza and Raymond Patriarca each had an eye toward whacking him, Sammy's date with death was hastened when he took on big Stevie Hughes as an enforcer for his money-lending business.

With the McLaughlin crew coming apart, Hughes may have seen Sammy as a reliable moneymaker, a safety net. Hughes had even asked Sammy for help in smoothing things over with the Winter Hill people. It's doubtful Sammy could've done much that way, since the Winter Hill Gang was already loading up to avenge the death of McLean. At six foot three and over 240 pounds, Hughes was an imposing figure. Some sources say that he, too, had done some boxing, but others say he wasn't especially tough. He was more comfortable hiding in the dark with a shotgun, his face covered by a stocking mask. But not even the enormous and homicidal Hughes could save Lindenbaum on that fateful afternoon on Route 114.

As soon as Sammy was dead, the local Italian faction raided his home. Their search turned up an envelope full of diamonds and $120,000 in cash. As vultures would pick the bones of a corpse, the Italian group promptly took over his loan-sharking business. Sammy's old clients may have thought they were off the hook when he was killed, but Patriarca's goons were soon visiting them.

Many different killers took credit for the assassination of Lindenbaum and Hughes. Some believe it was Barboza, but there are many good candidates. As the killer of Buddy McLean, Hughes was a big trophy for whoever whacked him. With Sammy Lindenbaum being a friend of the Charlestown clique, the old Bobbed Hair Bandit had to go too. A news photographer snapped a picture of the two dead men in the overturned car; they seemed to be huddled together in death, comforting each other as the life ran out of them.

Eddie Connors leaves a house flanked by Boston police in 1959. *The Boston Globe/Getty Images*

Eddie Connors:
The Man Who Knew Too Much

*Having Information Was One Thing. Talking about It
Was Another . . .*

Eddie Connors's body was found on the floor of a Morrissey
Boulevard phone booth. He'd been blasted in the chest with a shotgun, shot with a .38-caliber, and strafed with a carbine.

So much for small guns. Sometimes a killer wants to make a statement.

The murder took place on a June night in 1975. Take away the Sunoco
station across the street and the modern automobiles passing by and it
could've been a scene from a 1940s B movie. Connors was gunned down
like a film noir weasel that had talked too much.

Connors had owned the Bulldog Lounge in Dorchester, a popular pub
on Savin Hill Avenue that featured cheap drinks, egg-salad sandwiches,
and a band that played Irish music. On Sunday afternoons, the Bulldog
presented Golden Joe Baker, a chubby, bald Elvis Presley impersonator
from Fall River. Golden Joe was banging out dented fenders in a body
shop when he won four hundred bucks on a horse; he spent his win-
nings on an Elvis costume and took on a new career. Connors saw him
once and hired him on the spot. Golden Joe strangely complimented the
lounge's funky, dirty feel. It was a place where long-haired young men
sat elbow to elbow with aging townies. Former heavyweight contender

Tom McNeeley was the assistant manager, and other ex-boxers helped Connors with bartending shifts. It was also a favorite gathering place for South Boston's criminal element. Connors liked the bad guys. Maybe they liked him too. After all, he'd once been Eddie "The Bulldog" Connors, the "New England middleweight champion."

How Connors ended up murdered in a phone booth is a story that could've happened only in Boston during the 1970s.

Twenty years earlier he'd been a busy, if somewhat limited, Boston fighter. He had his good points in the ring. He was Irish, which helped sell tickets; he was from South Boston, which meant he had a dependable local following; he was an ex-Marine who had served in the Korean War, which made him a sentimental favorite; and he had what is known in the business as a "fan friendly" style. Of his twenty-two victories, eighteen had come inside the distance; ringside reporters used to say you could hear the "thwack" when Connors threw his straight right, like a baseball bat making contact. "I did a lot of sparring with Eddie Connors," said Eddie Grenke. "We were both inside fighters, so we liked to work out together. I'd say he was a bit on the slow side. That's why he liked to get in close so he could work the uppercut."

Rarely fighting outside the Boston bubble, Connors put up a record of 22-7-1. His career highlight came in April of 1959 when he headlined at the Garden against former welterweight champion Tony DeMarco.

DeMarco's career was in the ashes after losing twice by knockout to Virgil "Honeybear" Akins. The plan was to rebuild DeMarco in the eyes of the customers by matching him against some easy opponents. Connors, who had served as DeMarco's sparring partner years earlier, got the call.

The fight was well publicized. DeMarco was still popular, and the Boston press knew Connors as a durable guy with a good punch. DeMarco, who was accused of having a weak chin after his recent losses, assured the press that he'd chosen Connors specifically because he was a puncher. DeMarco wanted to prove his chin was sturdy. Connors did his part to sell the fight, predicting he'd knock DeMarco out. Later, Connors said his comments were merely the work of a publicity man.

What reporters didn't know was that DeMarco and Connors were friends. They even went to church together the morning of their fight and prayed that no harm would come to them during the contest. They wished each other luck and parted ways until fight time.

The first five rounds went by without much drama, but in the final moments of the sixth, DeMarco caught Connors with a combination to the head. Connors went down. Showing the bulldog toughness for which he was known, Connors got to his feet at a count of three. The rest of the fight was all DeMarco. The faded ex-champ busted open a cut over Connors's right eye in the ninth and, as the AP reported, "pounded him almost at will during the last two rounds."

By the bout's final minute, Connors was barely hanging on, glancing at the clock while the crowd of 8,053 screamed for DeMarco to put him away. DeMarco later said he wasn't looking to score a stoppage and wanted to go the full route. Chances are he'd allowed his friend to finish on his feet. After ten rounds, DeMarco won what the AP called "a convincing but unspectacular" decision. At the end, DeMarco admired Connors for going the distance with him. "He'd come a long way from being a sparring partner," DeMarco said. "I was proud of him."

Connors remained friends with DeMarco during the 1960s, when both were retired from boxing. They occasionally appeared together at charity events, and when DeMarco went into liquor sales, Connors was a steady buyer, keeping his tavern stocked with DeMarco's product. Years later, when DeMarco was operating a cocktail lounge in Phoenix, Connors sent him a film of their fight. As far as DeMarco knew, his old buddy and sparring partner was just a workingman looking after his customers. If Connors was involved with crooks, DeMarco looked the other way. "Eddie Connors's story hurt me," DeMarco said. "He was a pal."

Positioned behind the bar in a white apron, Connors seemed like a typical Irish American bartender right out of central casting. He had a wide, friendly face and a shock of wavy hair. He was successful enough that he opened a second establishment right across the street from the Bulldog. He was known as a great family man—he had seven children—and loved to work with neighborhood kids, whether it was hosting free pony rides at his home in Sharon, raising money for local Little League teams, or helping to send kids to summer camp.

Yet Connors has also been described as a career criminal, a wannabe who participated in the occasional robbery.

Enter James "Spike" O'Toole, the last key member of the McLaughlin crew. Just out of prison for assaulting an ex-cop, Spike started appearing in the Bulldog Lounge, drinking too much and running his mouth about wanting to whack Howie Winter, Somerville's top racketeer since the death of Buddy McLean. This may have been the ranting of a drunk, but O'Toole was a loose cannon, not to be ignored.

One evening Connors took it upon himself to warn Winter's crew, which included the soon-to-be-infamous Whitey Bulger, of O'Toole's presence. It was decided that O'Toole should be removed. Connors promised to call Winter when O'Toole was next in. On a December night in 1973, a drunken O'Toole came stumbling out of the tavern and into a blizzard of gunfire.

Why Connors inserted himself into Winter Hill business was unclear, though some suspected he simply wanted to be on their good side. There was talk that one of his business partners had once betrayed Winter Hill during the Boston gang war, and Connors may have been trying to show that he was a stand-up guy. The problem was that Connors started bragging about his part in O'Toole's murder. Word got back to Winter Hill that Connors was talking too much. Connors was also being investigated for his part in the recent robbery of an armored car, which allegedly involved Bulger and Winter. The concern grew that Connors was going to spill everything.

Connors should've seen his end coming. He received a call at the bar from Howie Winter. Something important was brewing, but Winter had to be discreet. Connors was told to speak to Winter from a pay phone so no one could hear the conversation. At the agreed-upon time, Connors drove his 1974 Lincoln Continental to a phone booth about a half mile from his tavern. He was waiting for the phone to ring when Bulger and Stephen Flemmi rose up like phantoms out of the weeds. They were armed to the teeth.

Connors landed with his head propped up against the glass, as if he'd simply fallen asleep in an uncomfortable position. The phone dangled by its cord just inches from his face. It hung there like a weird parody of the old microphones that were lowered down for ring announcers to introduce fighters. As he lay dead, it began to rain. The motor of his Lincoln was still running, the driver-side door still open.

Later, as detectives combed the area outside the booth, they found a piece of Eddie's jaw on the ground as well as his thumb. A policeman gathered up nine spent shotgun shells and put them in a McDonald's cup. He calmly told the *Globe* that Eddie's "chest and stomach are pretty much gone."

When a crowd formed, a cop threw a white sheet over the dead boxer's body. At 11:15 at night, a hearse arrived. The corpse was shoved into a green vinyl body bag and taken away. Detectives stayed behind, looking for clues among the spent shell casings and pieces of Eddie.

Tommy Tibbs on his way to his upset victory over
Willie Pep. *Bettman Archive/Getty Images*

Tommy Tibbs:
The Journeyman

He Could Beat Willie Pep, But He Couldn't Find Stardom . . .

He doesn't belong in this story. It doesn't make sense to include him. Then again, nothing about Tommy Tibbs made sense. His dedication to boxing was unparalleled, yet he never made it to the top of the business. And unlike most Boston fighters of the day, he fought all over the world. Strangest of all, he was on the wrong end of many scorecards, but he once won a split decision over the great Willie Pep.

Like many journeymen with long careers, the record that Tibbs left behind is both gargantuan and misleading. No opponent would call him a pushover. Yet his record of 60-77-4 is what happens to a fighter when he is good enough to go the distance with anybody but is constantly in someone else's hometown and can't land the big punches. In another example of how he didn't make sense, the powerfully built Tibbs was a shockingly ineffective hitter. In 141 professional bouts, he scored only 14 knockouts.

This power shortage, more than likely, was why he was such an attractive opponent whose services were required around the planet. If you had a young prospect but you didn't want him to risk getting hurt, or had an older fighter who needed a win, Tibbs was ideal. Since judges would always say they voted for the guy who threw the harder shots, a slapper like Tibbs would always be on the short end. That is, until he fought Pep.

At the time, Pep had 209 victories, had enjoyed two turns as featherweight champion, and though he was thirty-five years old with many miles behind him, he seemed as brilliant as ever. He had trouble getting television dates because of his age and size—the networks were more interested in young heavyweights than aging featherweights—which was why he took a lot of fights in Boston for Sam Silverman. On January 14, 1958, Pep was matched against Tibbs at the Mechanics Building in Boston. For Pep, it was just another chance to hit Boston for an easy payday.

"Don't let anyone tell you Pep was past his prime, either," said Jimmy Connors, who had dropped a decision to Pep at the Garden in December of 1957. "Pep would throw fifteen or sixteen punches at a time, all quick, and then he'd finish with a big right hand—boom! They say he couldn't punch, but he broke my nose and knocked a tooth out of my head. I liked him, though. He would say, 'Jimmy, we're in the same racket. I wish you well.'"

Eddie Spence remembers Pep another way. "He was the most foulmouthed man I ever met. Most fighters are quiet in the locker room, but Pep was nonstop, 'fuck this, fuck that.' I think Pep wanted us younger fighters to think he was a tough guy, or a street guy."

The matchup was a testament to how far Tibbs had come in a short time. Just a few years earlier he'd been taking fights for a sawbuck in Ohio, Kentucky, and Indiana. He was willing to fight anybody but didn't have the best luck. While fighting Johnny Cook in Huntington, West Virginia, he accidentally drank from an ammonia bottle between rounds and began choking so badly that the ring physician stopped the fight.

By 1952, he and his brother Freddie, who boxed as "Jimmy Montgomery," had relocated to Boston's Roxbury neighborhood and began working for Silverman. Tibbs quickly became Sam's most reliable workhorse, fighting across the New England circuit as often as five times per month. The losses piled up, but his career ignited after a trilogy of bouts with former champion Lauro Salas at Hollywood's Legion Stadium. Going 1-1-1 with Salas boosted Tibbs's confidence. He went on a rare winning streak, even scoring upset wins over highly regarded Lulu Perez and Frankie Ippolito. Tibbs had such momentum going that a few Boston sportswriters actually picked him to beat Pep, since the ex-champ was getting on in years and Tibbs had a newfound commitment to the business.

"Tommy was always in the New Garden Gym," said Connors. "I sparred with him many times. He was great to train with, because he was always in top shape and could go eight or nine rounds without getting tired. That's why he was always ready to take a fight on a moment's notice." During this period, Tibbs sparred with everyone from Tony DeMarco to Kid Gavilan to Sandy Saddler. As Connors recalled, "He didn't care if you were a featherweight or a heavyweight, he'd go eight rounds with you, and then another eight with someone else."

The Willie Pep that Tibbs fought in 1958 was a veritable storehouse of tricks. His favored strategy was to frustrate his opponents early, tie them up, and jab and grab until they grew desperate. Then, as they began to panic and throw wild shots, Pep could pick them apart and win the later rounds without much fuss. Tibbs, however, didn't panic and didn't grow frustrated. The crowd cheered Tibbs's every move and jeered Pep for grabbing too often. Even during the tenth and final round, which Pep dominated with left jabs and right crosses, the customers were clearly with Tibbs. The *Globe*'s John Ahern scored the bout for Pep by a point but noted that the veteran "couldn't seem to fathom the windmill motion" of Tibbs and spent the late rounds "backing up, searching for the opening that he couldn't find."

A ringside photographer caught the dramatic moment in the ninth when Pep lost his balance and fell; the scene appeared in newspapers and magazines for weeks, so rare was it for Pep to be off his feet. With more than four thousand customers watching, Tibbs stood over a surprised Pep and probably felt, for a rare time in his career, like the absolute ruler of the world. When the scorecards were turned in, Tibbs had won a ten-round split decision by the narrowest of margins. Pep wasn't happy with the scoring, but he gave Tibbs credit. "He's a good, strong kid," Pep said. "He'd give anybody a fight."

"It was very close," said Connors. "Willie was the type, even at that stage, where you had to press him. And Tommy stayed on him. But it was close. My friends and I thought Pep won, but it was a split decision for Tommy. That was ok. Tommy was robbed on a lot of close decisions. This time a close one went his way."

Tibbs was twenty-three at the time, a father of three, and a feel-good story for the local press. His weekend job selling newspapers at a down-town newsstand prompted more than one reporter to say the living legend Pep had lost to a Boston newsboy. But despite some temporary prestige, Tibbs's win over Pep didn't help his career. He lost his next seven fights. By the time he was stopped in five by Bert Somodio in Manila, it was as if the Pep fight never happened.

Despite a fear of flying, Tibbs spent the next few years taking bouts around the world. Fighting far from home, Tibbs found himself losing more close ones and being a victim of promoters skimming his purse to pay for publicity and other expenses. To make ends meet and feed his growing family, he took a variety of odd jobs, including welding at a steel plant and driving a cab.

In 1965, Boston police held Tibbs as a suspect in an armed robbery. Nothing came of the incident, and his career went on uninterrupted. In 1967, Tibbs complained of a neck injury and quit fighting.

"I don't know if Tommy had the right guidance," said Connors. "Managers and promoters in those days were all connivers. They could talk you into anything."

Five years later, in 1972, Silverman talked Tibbs into one last perfor-mance, a bout in Portland, Maine, against Bobby Richard. Tibbs, described by a *Lowell Sun* columnist as "a fat and pathetic fighter who no longer has any business in the ring," was stopped in the sixth. Officially, this was loss number seventy-seven. Now the father of seven, Tibbs worked as a boxing instructor at the Boston Parks Department.

On a Friday night in August of 1974, Tibbs was in the Plaza Café in Roxbury, arguing with a Dorchester man named Roberto Carr. As the quarrel escalated, Carr shot Tibbs in the chest four times with a .22-caliber revolver. Tibbs was taken to City Hospital where he died the next day. He was forty.

Tibbs had probably faced off with Carr the way he had faced men in the ring, as just another opponent. That he joined the long list of boxers killed in Boston was odd, though. He wasn't Irish or Italian. He wasn't part of a gang war. All he'd ever been was a workingman trying to feed his family. Carr was sentenced to ten years at Walpole state prison. During the trial he explained that he'd loaned Tibbs two dollars during a dice game. The argument had been about when Tibbs would return the loan. Tibbs was killed over two dollars. Like so much else about him, it just didn't make sense.

Paul Raymond, a star in two sports, couldn't resist the lure of Boston's streets. *The Boston Globe/ Getty Images*

Paul Raymond:
Heavyweight Homicide

*He'd Survived Ali and a Stint in the Marines,
but Not Boston's Deadly Streets . . .*

Paul Raymond was born August 22, 1942. He was a Somerville boy, growing up in the shadow of Winter Hill. He wasn't especially known for unlawful activity, but in December of 1974, three days before Christmas, he was killed during a shootout in Boston's North End.

He'd been booted out of the My Place lounge on Commercial Street at 2:30 in the morning. Angry and drunk, he went to his car and grabbed his pistol. Then he went back and killed the owner, Anthony Gioia. He also put a bullet in the hip of Gioia's brother Angelo. Unlucky for Raymond, Angelo was armed and fired back. Raymond's was the 129th murder in the city that year.

A standout football player at Somerville High School, Raymond found his real calling at local Golden Glove competitions in the late 1950s. He was a scrappy kid with a lot of energy, eager to learn as much as he could about boxing. He shined so brightly as an amateur that there was talk that he might go to the 1964 Olympic Games. But Raymond couldn't wait to turn pro. In December 1960, as part of a Boston Garden show where Joe Barboza lost a split decision to Bob Jasmin, Raymond won his professional debut by stopping Joe Hill in the first. He went on to knock out his first four opponents.

It was around this time that Raymond ran into the fists of Buddy McLean, already known as the top gangster of Winter Hill. Details of the event are murky, though it is generally believed that Raymond was involved in a bar fight over a woman and McLean somehow got involved. Naturally, like two bull elephants trying to establish their turf, Raymond and McLean started going at it. Depending on whose account you want to believe, Raymond either held his own or McLean picked him up like a lawn dart and threw him headfirst into a wall. However it ended, Raymond supposedly apologized to McLean and the two became friendly. Raymond later worked tending bar at McLean's favorite pub. Some sources say McLean even hired Raymond to work for his loan-sharking business.

Just as he was developing into a fighter, Raymond's career was interrupted by the war in Vietnam. He joined the Marines, injured his ankle while stationed in North Africa, and returned to civilian life with a permanent limp. So what did he do? He went back to boxing.

"He was crazy when he came back from the military," said Jerry Forte. "There was something off about Paul. A lot of his old friends stayed away from him."

By now he was a 190-pounder, solid, able to shove opponents around. He was a character, too. After dropping Paul Kasper in the first round with a left hook, Raymond stood in the neutral corner and demonstrated the winning punch for the Garden crowd. As Kasper was counted out, Raymond was still entertaining the ringsiders. "He was kind of a silly guy," said Forte.

Raymond became part of Sam Silverman's "Mod Squad," a group of young fighters so named because of their longish hair and their ability to draw younger audiences to Boston-area fights. That Raymond worked part-time as a bartender-bouncer at a joint in Somerville added to his charm.

Though Boston hosted far fewer boxing shows into the 1960s, Silverman saw new frontiers everywhere, bringing fights to New England towns that hadn't seen live boxing in decades. In July of 1969, Raymond went to Portland to fight Pete Riccitelli. It was a messy fight, marred by fouls in the ring and ringside brawls among spectators, but Raymond won a ten-round decision and the New England heavyweight title.

"If Sam had a fighter he wanted to promote and you were in his weight class, you could end up fighting him four or five times," said Eddie Spence. "But you were always happy to get the call from Sam. What people don't understand is that it wasn't always easy to get fights, especially if you were any good. You'd take anything that was offered. I fought Riccitelli five times in Portland, three times in one summer."

What kept fighters such as Spence and Raymond going was the novelty of being a big fish in an ever-diminishing pond.

"If you were a main-event fighter in New England," said Spence, "you were a celebrity. You did what celebrities did. People were always inviting you somewhere. It was like being in a rock band." Spence even recalled spectators rushing up to him after a fight to shove dollar bills into his glove.

With Spence and Raymond each having success in Portland, Silverman's next step was to match Raymond against Spence for those same Portland fans. Spence was an unusual specimen, a frail-looking young man who was studying psychology in upstate New York. He sang a little, too, and sometimes appeared in amateur stage productions. He also had a nice left hook recently taught to him by the great New York trainer, Freddie Brown. Armed with this new punch, the spindly Spence could slice a man's face like he was wielding a straight razor.

"I'd had thirty or forty fights before I learned how to throw a proper left hook," Spence said. "But I came back from New York and I was knocking the shit out of people. People would ask, 'Where'd you get that left hook?' I'd say, 'Freddie Brown.' Freddie said give him two years and he'd me make into a good professional fighter. I said, 'Two years?

Geez, I've already been at this a long time.' But at least he gave me a left hook."

In May of 1970, at the Expo Building in Portland, Spence put his new punch to work on Raymond and carved him up. Referee Pete Bennett took note of the damage to Raymond's face and stopped the bout at the end of the third. To lose by TKO was embarrassing for Raymond, since he had outweighed Spence by 27 pounds.

"He was strong," said Spence, "but not a very good puncher. He liked to get you against the ropes and wrestle you. His problem was that he had paper-thin skin. He was bleeding all over the place; every time I hit him I'd open a new cut, even on his neck under the ear. And it was a very rich, red blood. I was covered in it."

"That was the goriest, bloodiest fight I've ever seen," said Silverman at the time, "and I've been in the business forty years and have seen more fights than anyone else in the world."

Silverman's faith in Raymond wasn't shaken by the bloodbath in Portland. When Muhammad Ali returned from his more than three-year exile to fight Jerry Quarry in Atlanta, Silverman took advantage of the year's biggest boxing event by putting Raymond in a live card to accompany the Garden's closed-circuit telecast of the Ali–Quarry bout. In front of ten thousand customers, probably the largest gathering to ever see him fight, Raymond scored two knockdowns and stopped Henry Jeter at 2:58 of the third.

Raymond returned to the Garden two months later to win a ten-round decision over Spence. The bout drew a disappointing crowd of 2,853, but it allowed Raymond to get some redemption and regain the New England heavyweight title.

Though Silverman hoped to make Raymond into a regional attraction, Raymond announced that he was leaving boxing to attend college. By 1971, Raymond was working part-time as a truck driver and taking accounting classes at Bentley. He considered himself retired from fighting. "I've been a pro since 1960," he said around this time, "but have had only fifteen fights. I'm not really what you would call an experienced fighter."

His frustration was indicative of Boston's fight scene.

"Boston boxing was a mix of politics and incompetence," said Spence, decades later. "I knew some very good fighters who never got anywhere, all because of politics. The incompetence was in the training and managing. When I fought Paul Raymond, there'd been an agreement that he would come in at a certain weight, because I only weighed around 170. He showed up at the weigh-in 30 pounds heavier than me. No one said a word. That was the Boston incompetence."

Raymond received a call from Silverman in the fall of 1972. Though he'd been out of the ring for a while and considered himself retired from boxing, he was intrigued by Silverman's offer. Silverman wanted Raymond to take part in an exhibition with the most famous fighter on the planet.

Since his historic loss to Joe Frazier in 1971, Ali had been traveling the world fighting middling opponents. Silverman planned for Ali to box two rounds each with some local characters, including Raymond. Cynics weren't sure what Ali could gain from taking on Silverman's young, unknown heavyweights, but "The Greatest" assured the local media that the event was no joke. "This is a lot harder than sparring in the gym," Ali said of the public exhibition. "You don't really know the fighters. The crowd also wants blood, so you have to please the crowd and try not to hurt the other guy."

At a press luncheon to announce the exhibition, Raymond attempted to steal a chunk of the spotlight for himself. First, he called Ali by his old name—Cassius—which led to an exchange of words and a scuffle. This was routine stuff from the Ali playbook. To some, though, the little shoving match looked heated. Then, to the surprise of onlookers, Raymond reared back and took a swipe at Ali. It was Somerville hubris at its best. Or worst. "Ali could've knocked him out right there at the press conference," said Forte. "Or he could've used the exhibition as a way to get even. I think people were expecting it. But how would Ali look if he'd done that?"

Raymond continued his antics on fight night, futilely trying to outdo Ali in showmanship. Described by one local columnist as an "overweight bartender" Raymond trotted into the ring wearing a bright pink terry-cloth robe. He minced around, going for laughs. By now Raymond's hair was thinning, but he wore a nasty mustache that dripped down the sides of his mouth, all the better to scowl at Ali. Ali feigned anger too, but once the exhibition began, Ali toyed with Raymond, slapping him with jabs. Even though Raymond wore headgear and Ali wore oversized, twenty-ounce "pillow" gloves, at least one reporter described Raymond looking "dizzy" after one of Ali's flurries.

According to Somerville folklore, Raymond managed to get Ali on the ropes at one point and actually land a left, but no bartender with a limp was going to accomplish much against Ali. When the exhibition was over, Ali took the Garden microphone and went into his usual shtick, calling out Frazier and others. Raymond, pink robe and all, was forgotten. He later told the *Globe*, "It was an honor just being in the same ring with him."

The farce with Ali was Raymond's final appearance in the ring. He left the business with a record of 12-2-3 with seven knockouts.

Somerville men who knew Raymond in his prime still describe him as the toughest son of a bitch they ever met. They remember him jogging around town, limping but still putting in the roadwork. They recall his thunderous body shots and the way he'd cut off the ring. It was largely because of Raymond that the Somerville Boxing Club was established. One of his disciples, Norman Stone, would guide John Ruiz all the way to the WBA heavyweight title and a trilogy of bouts with Evander Holyfield. "Paul Raymond was my best friend," Stone said for a 2012 magazine interview.

The gossip about Raymond was that he developed a taste for drugs. He started to wander the streets in a stoned haze looking for trouble. He was said to have fantasies about avenging the death of Buddy McLean, who had been whacked a decade earlier. He was allegedly telling his buddies that he planned to go into sales, but by 1974 he seemed rootless, unsure of himself and his future. Drugs made him irrational.

"I think he became a different person," said Spence. "I didn't know him well, but I was aware that he came from a hard environment. I quit boxing after our second fight and moved to New York, but I would occasionally hear about Paul, usually from people four or five degrees removed, that he was hanging around with people he shouldn't have been around."

What made Paul Raymond go for his pistol that night in 1974? What prompted him to engage in a gun battle outside a North End restaurant? Was he simply high and drunk? Was it the same impulsiveness that made him take a swat at Ali during a press lunch or take on Buddy McLean in a bar? Was the fearlessness he'd always shown actually a sort of madness?

Maybe there was too much Somerville in his blood. Maybe he was still trying to impress all of those tough guys he'd heard about growing up. For guys like Paul Raymond, the legacy of Winter Hill was hard to escape.

Johnny Pretzie's boss Larry Zannino at Suffolk County Court, 1978. *The Boston Globe/Getty Images*

Johnny Pretzie:
Sharkey's Boy

*He Was Supposed to Be Boston's Next Boxing Star,
but Fate Had a Different Agenda . . .*

For Johnny Pretzie it ended with a gun blast to the face.

During the early morning hours of a Wednesday in July of 1989, police found Pretzie's body on Dorchester Street outside O'Leary's Pub in South Boston. Following a trail of bloody footprints that went to an apartment above O'Leary's, they found his killer, an off-duty housing authority officer named Richard Geary. A thirty-three-year-old who worked part-time at O'Leary's as a bouncer, Geary said that he'd shot Pretzie in self-defense. Geary explained that Pretzie, the crazy fucker, was drunk and coming at him. Sure, Pretzie was nearly seventy, but any of O'Leary's regulars would tell you that Pretzie was a bully and a maniac. He'd once been a heavyweight boxer and he liked to pick fights with people because he knew he could knock them out. Geary said that he hadn't meant to kill Pretzie and was sorry that he died. "But what the hell," he said. "I did Southie a favor."

The press made a big deal of Pretzie's background as a boxer, particularly the fact that he'd been in the ring with some famous names, including Rocky Marciano and Jake LaMotta. There was no mention that Pretzie was friendly with some of the city's most repulsive criminals.

Born John Pretzian in Cambridge but raised in Boston's Back Bay neighborhood, Pretzie had been an amateur star before the war. Though his Armenian parents didn't care for Pretzie's interest in pugilism, he seemed made for fighting; he had a good left hand, a rugged physique, and a readiness to brawl. He squashed the competition, winning more than thirty bouts, all by knockout. When he turned down a chance to play semipro baseball in the Eastern Shore League to focus on fighting, it appeared Boston had a true ring hero in the making. The highlight of his amateur career was winning the heavyweight laurels at a December 1942 event called the "All America Tournament." He beat two opponents in the same night, one of them in only thirty seconds.

Former heavyweight champion Jack Sharkey ("The Boston Gob") refereed the All America contests and took notice of Pretzie, commenting that the youngster was a bit crude but had potential. "Pretzie will be a good heavyweight to have around," Sharkey told the *Globe*. "He's willing to get in there and throw punches. And he has plenty of color." Pretzie's final amateur bout before leaving for military duty was hyped in the papers as a last chance to see a genuine Boston attraction. He had become, the *Globe* noted, amateur fandom's "pet of the season."

After three years in the U.S. Army Air Corps, Pretzie returned to Boston in 1945 and embarked on a professional boxing career. Because of his amateur success, Pretzie didn't start out in backwaters like Fall River or in faraway Providence. His early bouts were in Boston venues, and Boston newspapers praised him as a budding, if somewhat clumsy, star in the making. He earned a bit of notoriety when he was spotted at Johnny Buckley's gym sparring with heavyweight contender Lou Nova and earned even more press thanks to his friendship with Peter Fuller, another young fighter who happened to be the son of Massachusetts Governor Alvan Fuller.

Interest in Pretzie skyrocketed when Sharkey officially signed on as his trainer and adviser. Pretzie was soon touted in the news as "Sharkey's boy," but it didn't take long for Sharkey to grow suspicious of his protégé.

Pretzie seemed lazy, showing up at the gym whenever he pleased. Sharkey was candid, telling the *Globe* that Pretzie had "a fat head," had been given too much attention too soon, and was more interested in hanging out in dance halls than fighting. Despite a few early victories, Pretzie remained rough, unpolished. He got worse with every fight. Sharkey severed ties with him within a year or so. After a decision loss to Ernie Griffin, the *Globe* called Pretzie "pitiful."

In 1949, Pretzie was matched in Rhode Island with Marciano, at the time an inexperienced slugger from Brockton. An out-of-shape Pretzie, having taken the fight on short notice, was knocked to the canvas four times before the bout was finally stopped in the fifth round. He later alleged that Marciano's camp had given him orders before the bout; if Marciano was cut, Pretzie was supposed to back off and fall the first time he was hit.

Whether Pretzie had been instructed to take a dive, his career sank after fighting Marciano. He lost his next six fights in a row, five by knockout. On March 11, 1954, he found himself in West Palm Beach to face LaMotta. The Bronx Bull had been out of the ring for more than a year and needed a pigeon.

Ticket-buyers knew from the first minute that something wasn't kosher. As LaMotta and Pretzie went through the motions, fans at the American Legion Arena began booing. Some simply got up and left. Unconcerned about the remaining customers yelling "fake," Pretzie kept flopping to the canvas. The debacle was finally stopped at 1:42 of the fourth. It would be Pretzie's last bout. He retired with a record of 9-14-1.

The Florida boxing commission reprimanded both Pretzie and LaMotta for what was described as a "poor showing," while ticket-buyers complained that Pretzie fell from punches that hadn't seemed especially damaging. Though there was no investigation, the arena's chairman Julian Field contacted the National Boxing Association and claimed LaMotta and Pretzie "did not bring credit to the boxing profession." Decades later, after he'd had a few drinks, Pretzie alluded to friends that he had been brought in from Boston to throw the fight, to "do business." "I was supposed to make him look good," Pretzie allegedly said. "It wasn't easy making Jake LaMotta look good."

Pretzie went on to live a kind of double life. For the next three decades, he worked with kids and was known as a decent guy, a boon to his community, a lovable boxing coach in Southie, a respected prison guard at Walpole. He preached clean living. He loved animals. He even did a little modeling. When Boston's Shawmut Bank needed an actor to portray their corporate symbol, "Chief Obbatinewat," in a television campaign, Pretzie was fitted with braids and war paint.

Pretzie also enjoyed the company of gangsters. More than one of the young boxers he'd trained worked as enforcers for Whitey Bulger. It wasn't unusual for Pretzie to be invited to gangster weddings in South Boston and seated alongside various killers, including Bulger and Stephen Flemmi. In time, Pretzie became a caricature of these psychopaths—he started carrying a gun and speeding around the city in his Trans-Am, drinking booze from a brown bag as he drove. He even created a hand signal known as "the Southie Wave," a variation of the "Hook 'em Horns" from the University of Texas. To Pretzie's delight, Whitey and the Southie crew started using it.

Pretzie's fascination with gangsters may have dated back to when he worked as a bouncer at a North End bar called The Bat Cove. The job required Pretzie to wear a Batman costume. No one thought a guy in a cowl and cape could be taken seriously, but more than one troublemaker got beat up and tossed by Pretzie in his guise as the caped crusader. It was also believed by Pretzie's family that the club's owner, Ilario Zannino (aka Larry Baione), sometimes hired Pretzie for dirtier jobs. Zannino's background included being part of a "pay or die" ring that landed him a stint in prison for extortion. A high-ranking figure in the Boston Mob, Zannino may have used Pretzie's muscle in his shakedown racket.

Many claim the turning point for Pretzie came when he got involved with a much younger woman known only as "Robin." Pretzie's family never approved of her—she was a cunning barfly described by one of his family members as a "Roslindale skank"—and her time with Pretzie was marked by violent arguments and police interventions. In January of 1988, Pretzie threw her from a second-floor window. She survived. He was given two years of probation. The star-crossed romance ended when Robin eventually drank herself to death.

Pretzie always had a cruel streak, which worsened as he aged. Friends described him as a nice guy who could suddenly turn vicious. His favorite trick was to lure people into fighting him. Not suspecting the old-timer could do much damage, gullible drunks would soon be knocked flat, their mouths bloody. Something as simple as interrupting his conversation could earn you a punch on the jaw. Maybe Pretzie's failure as a boxer caused him to pick on soft-chinned civilians. His bullying reputation followed him all the way to Geary's murder trial.

At Suffolk Superior Court in December of 1989, jurors listened to a tale of how Geary followed Pretzie into the parking lot after O'Leary's had closed and shot him point-blank in the face with a .38-caliber revolver. The prosecution described Pretzie as drunk and defenseless, while Geary's attorney relied on Pretzie's violent past to bolster the argument that Geary had acted in self-defense. Geary insisted he'd shot Pretzie because he feared the ex-heavyweight was reaching for his own weapon. In fact, when Pretzie's sister Marion was phoned and told there'd been a death, her first thought was that her madman brother had finally killed someone. In the end, despite Pretzie's beastly reputation, the jury found Geary guilty of second-degree murder.

Decades have passed since Pretzie was killed, but there is still no general consensus as to what sort of man he was. Some called Pretzie a Jekyll and Hyde type, a perfectly polite man by day but a terror by night. His loved ones found excuses for him, that it was Robin's fault that he started drinking, that Geary had been a coward, embarrassed that an old man had beaten him up. All that is certain is that Pretzie was another boxer killed on a Boston street. Considering the way he behaved in his later years, maybe getting shot in the face was inevitable.

Whitey Bulger's South Boston liquor store. Bulger liked to hire boxers as henchmen. *The Boston Globe/Getty Images*

Frankie MacDonald:
South Boston's Hope

*The Entire Neighborhood Turned Out to Say
Farewell to Frank the Tank . . .*

F rankie MacDonald was born on November 24, 1959, just as "Mack the Knife," Bobby Darin's hit song about a murderer, was enjoying another week at the top of the Billboard charts. In July of 1984, MacDonald was found dead at twenty-four, shot in the back and left in an abandoned car, his head covered by trash bags.

Darin's old recording, with its lyrics about bodies oozing life, could have been an anthem for MacDonald's South Boston neighborhood. The song's main character, a charming killer named Macheath, could have been a stand-in for Whitey Bulger, the Machiavellian devil who pumped drugs into the area as young people like MacDonald fell sway.

It's not to trivialize MacDonald's death by mentioning it alongside a bouncy old pop tune, but like Mackie's victims who seemed to disappear in the dark, MacDonald didn't stand a chance.

The early reports of his death depicted MacDonald as a confused young man who'd had some brushes with the law. This didn't sound like "Frank the Tank," the best amateur boxer South Boston had seen in years, a brawny slugger who needed nothing more than a few body shots to leave an opponent crushed on the canvas.

Of course, not many knew about the all-night parties at his apartment. At one time, passersby could look up at his window on the third floor and see Frankie shadowboxing in the kitchen. But at night, the shades were drawn while he and his buddies snorted up hills of cocaine. He was supposed to fight his way out of the Old Colony housing project where he'd grown up, but in the months before his death he'd seemed more interested in cocaine than boxing.

Frankie MacDonald grew up in Southie's Old Colony project, a place so bleak that politicians used it as an example of how public housing had failed. In those years of race riots and rampant crime, the media fixated on Southie as a neighborhood of drug dealers, dumpster fires, and poverty-stricken bigots. It must've seemed that everyone in the world was against Southie. It's no wonder the locals treated Bulger as a kind of Robin Hood figure. In his memoir about life in South Boston, Frankie's brother Michael wrote of Bulger, "He was our king, and everyone made like they were connected to him in some way."

Bulger, who had survived the Irish gang wars to become the city's top mobster, often hired local boxers to help with his ever-expanding empire. Howie Carr of the *Boston Herald* once noted, "Ex-boxers always seemed to end up in the rackets in Boston, and they seemed to have a much higher mortality rate than hoodlums who hadn't made it to the Golden Gloves." Even ex-pugs who didn't get killed seemed to have bad things happen, like Dorchester middleweight Mickey Dwyer. Representing his South Boston crime buddies, the feisty Dwyer once ran afoul of gangster Kenny Killeen in Southie's Transit Café. Dwyer's ability to hook off a jab meant nothing; Killeen shot him in the arm and bit his nose off.

Bulger lingered around Southie's boxing gyms, always on the lookout for tough guys who might be molded into enforcers. He'd tell the kid that boxing was a dead end, and more money could be made on the street selling drugs. It's astonishing that so many fighters gave up their careers to join Whitey's dirty army of drug dealers and killers, but the slick-talking

Bulger could convince you that sports were just a way for adults to stay in a childhood sandbox.

John "Red" Shea, another South Boston fighter turned criminal, said that Bulger could be shockingly blunt on the subject. When Shea said he wanted to pursue a boxing career, Bulger scoffed and said, "Boxing's for niggers." Shea, who'd had some professional bouts and had even worked as a sparring partner for lightweight champion Sean O'Grady, signed on with Bulger and eventually served twelve years in prison for cocaine trafficking. Kevin Weeks was from the same neighborhood as Frankie MacDonald and came from a boxing family; he ended up as one of Bulger's enforcers. He served time, too. Edward MacKenzie, who had done some amateur boxing, described his first encounter with Bulger as a kind of spiritual encounter: "I'd spent so much time proving I was the toughest of the tough. But once I met Whitey, I understood that all of my toughness would somehow be laid at his feet."

In the presence of Bulger, these young fighters became like little boys trying to impress an adult with how much weight they could lift or how high they could jump. As Weeks noted in his memoir, working for Bulger "carried a lot of prestige. My father was pleased that I was working for the top gangster in the city." Freddie Roach, who would go on to train such stars as Manny Pacquiao, Johnny Tapia, and James Toney, once told Yahoo Sports that as a teen he had done landscaping work at Bulger's home in Milton. The teen Roach was blissfully unaware of his employer's background, knowing him only as "a really nice guy" who sponsored local amateur teams. "He always treated us very well," Roach said.

Around the same time that Roach was trimming Bulger's hedges, Frankie MacDonald had started boxing at McDonough's Gym on East Fourth Street. Bulger lingered in the shadows of the gym like a vampire, watching him. He kidded with Frankie. He said he could use Frankie as a bodyguard, a line he probably used on a hundred different kids. Every kid in Southie wanted to be noticed by Bulger. But Frankie wouldn't take the bait.

Frankie didn't want to be associated with criminals. Just recently a former Golden Gloves winner, George "Skippy" Cream, had been killed in a shootout with Gloucester police. Cream was yet another poor kid from a tough neighborhood who got mixed up in drugs and petty crime. His death at twenty-seven should've been a warning to Frankie to stay out of trouble.

Furthermore, Frankie's family had been through enough tragedies without him getting involved with Bulger. Ever since Frankie's alcoholic father abandoned them, the MacDonalds of Patterson Way seemed to be under the darkest of dark clouds. One of Frankie's brothers was locked away as a schizophrenic; another brother committed suicide by leaping from a rooftop. A sister fell, or was pushed, from a rooftop and was never the same. His younger brother, Kevin, was enmeshed in Southie's crime culture. Just months after Frankie's death, Kevin hanged himself in a prison cell.

Unfortunately, Frankie found it impossible to stay off of Bulger's radar. For one thing, the two men working his corner throughout his amateur career were a couple of Bulger's henchmen, Paul "Polecat" Moore, and Tommy Cronin. For another, Frankie's brother Kevin had been selling cocaine on the street from an early age, knowing that his earnings were likely being funneled upward to the main man. Inevitably, Kevin's shady connections got Frankie into trouble. The police raided the apartment they shared and found an unlicensed shotgun and ten hits of acid under Frankie's bed. This was Kevin's stash, but Frankie wouldn't rat on his brother. The courts made a deal with Frankie. He could avoid jail if he did a hitch in the Marines. He agreed. When he got out, he resumed boxing. Somehow, he seemed even bigger and more destructive than before.

In 1983, Frankie was on a winning New England Golden Gloves team that included a burly teenager from New York. The outsider's name was Mike Tyson. The group photo that appeared in newspapers is odd—Tyson is the only African American on the team, and he's grinning wildly. The rest of the team are dour, particularly Frankie. In what should've been a proud moment, he's looking away, distracted, uninterested, as if the heaviness of the Old Colony projects prohibited any real glee. Frankie, wrote Steve Marantz of the *Globe*, "was a quiet young man . . . never opening a window on his private thoughts."

Yet, all seemed well in Frankie's world. He'd been hired as a sparring partner for middleweight contender Sean Mannion, and it was rumored that noted trainer Lou Duva would help Frankie turn pro. Frankie was living the dream, driving around the city in his Lincoln and working part-time as a bouncer at The Rat, a notorious Kenmore Square club that featured punk and new-wave bands. He was also enjoying his fame as a local boxer. He told his younger brothers that someday he'd be so rich that he'd get them all out of Southie and buy them homes in Florida. Down there, he said, the weather was always warm and kids could go to Disney World whenever they wanted. It was a good dream to have. Then it all changed. He was scheduled to make his professional debut, but he unexpectedly canceled. His behavior became weird, erratic, a sure sign that drugs had overtaken him. He'd disappear for weeks at a time.

One night at Frankie's apartment, a plan was hatched to rob a Wells Fargo truck. Kevin was supposed to be involved, but he balked. Suddenly, Frankie offered to step in and take Kevin's place. Maybe being around criminals all his life made it seem natural to get involved in a crime.

It could also be that Frankie MacDonald was never as straitlaced as he'd pretended to be. It's not as if he'd never done anything wrong; he had at least one assault charge, and just months earlier he'd been charged with possession of burglary tools. Perhaps coke had altered his judgment.

Or maybe he'd come to believe Bulger's line that crime paid better than boxing.

Whatever the reason, Frankie wanted to be part of the robbery.

According to legend, Kevin and Frankie got into an argument that night. They ended up in the street outside their apartment throwing punches at each other. Who should drive up in a big car? It was Bulger. The Sultan of Southie allegedly told them to stop fighting. It didn't look

SLAUGHTER IN THE STREETS

good, he said, for brothers to fight. Kevin got in the car with Bulger. Frankie walked away. Did it really happen this way? Bulger sidekick Kevin Weeks swore it did.

On Tuesday morning, July 17, 1984, Frankie and two companions robbed an armored truck on Mystic Avenue in Medford. Things almost went according to plan until the driver, Joseph Gesualdo, shot Frankie in the back. Frankie reportedly made his way to the getaway car. His pals stuffed him underneath the seats as if to hide him. That's where he supposedly bled to death. Later, the coroner told Frankie's mother that her son had also been strangled. There were finger marks on his neck, and his face was deeply reddened from busted capillaries. The theory went that his partners in the heist worried that once he got to a hospital he'd give away their names, so they killed him right there in the car. It was also reported that Frankie's fingerprints had been burned off with acid to hide his identity.

Frankie's mother boldly approached Bulger on the street and asked if he knew anything about the robbery. Bulger offered his condolences but declared he knew nothing about the incident in Medford. Of course, Bulger's innocence was unlikely since his motto was, "Nobody shits in my backyard without me knowing about it." A short time later, a South Boston man opened a new clam restaurant. Some believed he had masterminded the robbery and had opened his clam shack with money from the job that cost Frankie MacDonald his life.

Many South Boston gangsters attended the wake. Children and relatives and cocaine dealers reminisced about Frankie's fights, and soon Jackie O'Brien's Funeral Parlor was alive with people shadowboxing, acting out Frankie's great moments. To the side of the room was a coffin filled with Irish trinkets gathered from the annual St. Paddy's Day parade, rosary beads, Irish flags, and the like. Also in it lay the body of Francis Xavier MacDonald, the best fighter South Boston had seen in years. At one point his mother jumped on the casket and began wailing; it took a few gangsters to pull her off. As the clamor increased, Frank the Tank lay peacefully, wrapped in his purple boxing robe.

Whitey Bulger and Stephen Flemmi were later
implicated in the murder of Eddie Connors. *The
Boston Globe/Getty Images*

CHAPTER 16

Ghosts of Winter Hill

Is the Story Really Over?

A s if the last century couldn't conclude without one more Boston fighter getting killed, there was David Stivaletta's death by gunshot in 1999. A highly touted amateur welterweight of the 1970s, Stivaletta was killed during an argument in the North End. He collapsed right around the corner from the Old North Church on a Sunday afternoon, in front of stunned sightseers shopping for pastry. Stivaletta was forty-two, a drug abuser, and known to local law enforcement as a troublemaker. The original reports said the altercation had been over a car accident. The shooter, a North Ender named David Pepicelli, claimed he had acted in self-defense. Pepicelli was eventually found guilty of involuntary manslaughter.

Stivaletta had been a second-generation boxer, his father Paul having been a moderately successful middleweight back in the early 1960s. Paul spent many years as Joe DeNucci's sparring partner and later applied for a promoter's license. His hope was to arrange a fight for Sonny Liston in Boston. By the 1970s, he was watching his son blossom into a fine amateur boxer. David was good enough at age fifteen that he was selected to represent New England at the National AAU Junior Olympics in

SLAUGHTER IN THE STREETS

South Carolina. He lost in the finals, but there was no reason to think he wouldn't follow his dad's footsteps into a professional boxing career. But the only tradition David carried on was the one where Boston fighters were shot and killed.

The Stivaletta case attracted attention because it had happened in broad daylight in front of witnesses, and the trial was drawn out for years. That it happened in the North End, a once-volatile area that had gone relatively quiet, also assured it some coverage. What went unnoticed was how much it had in common with certain stories from the past. The shooting wasn't far from where Frankie Wallace met his end, or Endicott Street where Sparky Chiampa had lived. Found near Stivaletta's death scene was a blood-soaked paper bag with a revolver in it, recalling Punchy McLaughlin's final moments. Stivaletta's decline from once-promising fighter to barroom brawler and substance user recalled the downfalls of Pretzie and Raymond and Frank the Tank. That the argument had been over a fender bender was as dumb as Tibbs being shot over a two-dollar loan. There were even murmurs that both Pepicelli and Stivaletta had links to organized crime.

But as much as Stivaletta's death felt like a touch of the old days, it was more of an anomaly than a hint of things to come.

By the early 2000s, Boston had changed. Silverman and Valenti were long dead, and no one seemed to know how to carry on the tradition of promoting fights. You'd be told that boxing was still vital—after all, women had taken it up—but neighborhood kids no longer peeked in gym windows hoping to see a DeMarco or a DeNucci. The Garden was torn down, rebuilt, and bought by a bank. Garden crowds were paying outrageous prices to see hockey or basketball or a concert. A few enterprising souls have tried to promote bouts, including members of the Valenti family, but the number of major boxing shows at the Garden since 2000 could be counted on the fingers of Punchy McLaughlin's fake hand.

The old boxing gyms morphed into modern facilities where office workers exercised in spandex tights and fretted over their body-fat ratios.

In the East Boston neighborhoods where Joe Barboza and his crew once roamed, a refurbished third-floor apartment is now a condo going for a half-million bucks. Tourists wander the North End, unaware that it was once a breeding ground for boxers and hoodlums. Southie, too, is unrecognizable from the bad old days.

Whitey Bulger, who would eventually land in a West Virginia prison where he was killed, spent the early 2000s on the lam, his role as an informant known to all. As Bulger's legend grew, his henchmen published ghostwritten memoirs. It seemed anyone who ever snorted a line of coke in Southie was granted a book deal. Now and then the names of Boston's murdered fighters came up, but they were part of the dim past, as anonymous as background characters in an old movie. Strangely, it was the specter of Eddie Connors that hovered around Boston. Like no other murdered fighter, Connors kept coming back to haunt.

More than two decades had passed since Connors was murdered, but he was mentioned frequently during the seemingly endless trials and testimonies of John Martorano. During his turn as an informant, Martorano confessed to driving the getaway car when Bulger and Flemmi killed Connors in a phone booth. Martorano, who was involved in twenty or so murders, received leniency for ratting. As the media was engulfed in Bulger mania, Martorano enjoyed a book deal and appearances on television. He philosophized about being a hired killer. He said he wasn't such a bad man. He was just doing a job. He said his priest forgave him. Most didn't fall for Martorano's shit, though he sold the movie rights to his life story for a quarter of a million bucks.

Connors came up again when Bulger, now eighty-three, went on trial in 2013. The prosecutors showed the jury a photo of Connors's butchered body. Bulger's lawyer objected. Such gruesome images, he said, could unfairly affect a juror's decision.

But for all of the memories Connors was bringing up, there wasn't much said about his past as a boxer, that he'd had a good right hand, or that he went ten hard ones with DeMarco at the Garden.

The trouble of ex-boxers wasn't news anymore, not the way it used to be.

• • •

When asked why so many Boston-area fighters found themselves lured into criminal life, Tony DeMarco gave a simple answer: "The glamour."

"I knew people with good jobs who secretly wanted to be with the wise guys," DeMarco said. One of his childhood buddies was Ronnie Cassesso, who was part of Barboza's crew. DeMarco never comprehended Ronnie the Pig's fixation on criminal life.

"It was difficult to understand," he said. "Ronnie had a good job. He was a heavy machine operator. He had a skill that not many North Enders had, and he made a good living. But he'd always wanted to be a wise guy."

Ronnie the Pig, one of the many men imprisoned after Barboza's testimony, sat on death row for five years. When Massachusetts abolished the death penalty, his sentence was changed to a life term in Walpole State Prison. He died in 1991. He'd had the unusual distinction of being buddies with both Tony DeMarco and Joe Barboza.

DeMarco has endured. He's still alive as of this writing. In recent years he was honored with a statue of his likeness in the North End, and an induction into the International Boxing Hall of Fame in the "Old-Timers" category. He and Rip Valenti have had streets named after them. He embraces his role as the humble little North Ender who became a champion and has spent many decades milking his little bit of fame. Not a year goes by where he isn't honored somehow, at an Italian men's club or an amateur boxing event. He was the welterweight champion for only a bit longer than two months, but people of a certain age still remember him as a major local figure, a one-man franchise. He'll tell you about the time he met Sammy Davis Jr., or the night he beat Saxton at the Garden, and the swarming parade of people that greeted him the next morning at his North End home. He won't say much about the Mob. There's always a sense that he knows more than he lets on and that he doesn't want his own achievements to be overshadowed by too much gangster talk. "There are nicer topics," he'll say. Ironically, DeMarco spent part of the early 2000s performing in a dinner-theater production where he played, of all things, a Mafia boss.

Joe DeNucci died in 2017. After his boxing career, he turned to politics; he earned accolades as the longest-serving state auditor in the history of Massachusetts. In 2008, while sitting for a magazine interview, the subject of murdered Boston fighters came up. Why had so many of them gone into a life of crime?

"Truthfully," he said, "I never considered them to be real fighters. They may have had some fights, but they weren't really fighters."

Reminded that he had been friendly with so many of the fighters who were eventually whacked—Barboza, Sacramone, DiSeglio, Connors, —he shrugged.

"I'll tell you something about the day Rocco was killed," DeNucci said. "The radio announced that a Newton fighter had been found dead. So my phone starts ringing off the hook. People thought it was me that was killed, because I was a Newton fighter. They were calling my family all day, just to make sure I was ok. It was crazy."

• • •

With a tale so grim, it's tempting to end things with a laugh. So here goes.

There's an anecdote about a Boston fighter that may or may not be factual. It was heard in the course of writing this book, and while it can't be verified—and no one who tells it wants to be credited—it's worth repeating.

The fighter was a good Boston middleweight who convinced his criminal buddies to let him take part in a routine robbery. (Sometimes, as the tale is told, it was a bank robbery; other times it was a store.) The fighter's job was to climb a tree and be a lookout. If he saw a police car, he was to wave at his buddies as a signal to stop their mission and scram. But as the fighter waited, he lost his balance and fell out of the tree. A bank clerk saw him fall and called the police. "A man has fallen out of a tree outside," the clerk said. A police cruiser was on the scene just as the fighter was shinnying back up to his perch. The robbers, seeing the police, panicked and left the scene. It's not known if the cops asked the fighter what he was doing in the tree or how he explained himself.

Whether or not the story is true, it says a lot.

And it probably is true.

• • •

It's tantalizing to wonder if Boston could generate such a relationship between fighters and gangsters today. The answer is probably no. For one thing, we'd need some fighters and gangsters, and the city hasn't been producing many of either.

But nothing is impossible.

At the time of Bulger's conviction in 2013, a number of optimistic editorials appeared in local newspapers declaring Boston was now too wealthy and sophisticated to ever again fall prey to such a monster. One op-ed piece in the *Globe* offered, "The best way to celebrate the fall of Whitey Bulger is to acknowledge his irrelevance to the Boston of today."

But these editorials came off as wishful thinking. With the FBI putting its focus on terrorism and international drug cartels, the chances for organized crime to flourish in some forgotten Boston neighborhood increase, and a new Bulger, or Buccola, could easily emerge. Only now he'll be Russian, or Brazilian, or Cape Verdean, or Asian. Why couldn't he find a couple of boxers to follow him? The lure of easy money will always be strong. There will always be knuckleheads. There will always be temptation.

And more than a century after Tommy Young was found slashed to death in East Boston, it could start all over again.

Was it always just a fluke of geography, with boxers and criminals coming from the same Boston communities? Was it just a case of neighborhood friends sticking together? Were the fighters actually criminals at heart, and once their boxing career was done they simply leaned on what they'd always known best? Were they simply naïve young guys buying into a game they couldn't possibly win? Or did they think their toughness in the ring would make them impervious to bullets? Did the fighters, perhaps weary of being at the mercy of managers, trainers, promoters, and the scale, see gangsters as a symbol of freedom, of doing as you pleased and damn the consequences?

The Boston boys who took up boxing were looking for more or less the same thing as the boys who went into crime. They'd wanted adventure, some fame, and a way to improve their lot in life. They were risk takers, and the risks were worth it. For poor kids living in unheated North End apartments or roach-infested Southie tenements, boxing and crime offered ways out. If a boxer–Mob link happened now, it wouldn't be in the North or South End, and the mobsters wouldn't be Irish or Italian, but it would work along the same lines as described by Jimmy Connors, a Boston fighter who fought Willie Pep and still thinks well enough of murderous Joe Barboza to say, "God bless him."

"You'd always hear that some fighter was hanging around with these guys," said Connors, no relation to Eddie. "The bad guys can see a vulnerable fighter from a mile away, you know. Fighters are like anyone else; they get swept up."

Connors never felt the allure, though. "I lived in New Bedford. I only went to Boston to train, or fight, and then I went home."

But he was in the city often enough to witness the sneaky ritual that went on between boxers and crooks, a strange little dance he saw time and time again. "The wise guy thinks the fighter might have some money. At the same time, the fighter thinks the wise guy has some money." Without humor, he added, "Most of the time, neither one had anything."

ACKNOWLEDGMENTS

I interviewed Tony DeMarco for *The Ring* magazine back in the early 2000s. I got to know Tony, and I was one of the many writers he invited to help with his autobiography, which was published in 2011 as *Nardo: Memoir of a Boxing Champion*. It was through Tony that I met Joe DeNucci. I interviewed DeNucci for *The Ring* in 2008, and we became friendly. "Da Nooch" invited me back to his State House office for lunch now and then, and we had several interesting conversations about the subjects mentioned in this book. Tony also introduced me to Lou Lanci, a good man who helped me understand the old North End.

More recently, I have to thank to Jimmy Connors, Jerry Forte, Eddie Grenke, and Eddie Spence, a quartet of Boston fighters who gave me a vivid picture of what New England boxing was like during the 1950s and 1960s. Thanks to Dan Cuoco for putting me in touch with them.

ABOUT THE AUTHOR

Don Stradley is an award-winning writer whose work has appeared in various publications, including *The Ring*, *Ringside Seat*, and ESPN.com. Along with his boxing coverage, he's written about baseball, NASCAR, and professional wrestling. Past books include *Berserk*, a biography of Edwin Valero and the first installment in the Hamilcar Noir series; *Schooled*, a dual biography of Lebron James for Scholastic; and a chapter in *The Ultimate Book of Boxing Lists* by Bert Sugar and Teddy Atlas. When not writing about sports, he's written about the movies for such magazines as *Cinema Retro* and *Noir City*.

SELECTED BIBLIOGRAPHY

Along with the Associated Press and the United Press, the following periodicals were used while writing this book: *The Boston Globe*, *The Boston Post*, *Fitchburg Sentinel*, *The Lowell Sun*, New York *Daily News*, *Syracuse Herald*, and *The Acton Assabet Valley Beacon*. Also, I have to express my appreciation for articles by Springs Toledo for the *City Journal* and George Hassett for *Dig Boston*.

Books

Carr, Howie, *Hitman—The Untold Story of Johnny Martorano: Whitey Bulger's Enforcer and the Most Feared Gangster in the Underworld*, New York, Forge Books, 2011.

English, T. J. *Paddy Whacked: The Untold Story of the Irish Gangster*, New York, ReganBooks, An Imprint of HarperCollins Publishers, 2005.

Fopiano, Willie, and John Harney, *The Godson: A True-Life Account of 20 Years Inside the Mob*, New York, St. Martin's Press, 1993.

Ford, Beverly, and Stephanie Schorow, *The Boston Mob Guide: Hit Men, Hoodlums, and Hideouts*, Charleston, South Carolina, The History Press, 2011.

Leavitt, Larry, *Loved and Feared: Buddy McLean, Boss of the Notorious Winter Hill Gang During Boston's Irish Mob War*, Strategic Book Publishing & Rights Co., 2019.

Lehr, Dick, and Gerard O'Neill, *Black Mass: The True Story of an Unholy Alliance between the FBI and Irish Mob*, New York, Perennial, An Imprint of HarperCollins Publishers, 2001.

Lehr, Dick, and Gerard O'Neill, *Whitey: The Life of America's Most Notorious Mob Boss*, New York, Broadway Books, 2013.

MacDonald, Michael Patrick, *All Souls: A Family Story from Southie*, Boston, Beacon Press, 1999.

MacKenzie, Edward J. Jr., and Phyllis Karas, *Street Soldier: My Life as an Enforcer for Whitey Bulger and the Boston Irish Mob*, Hanover, New Hampshire, Steerforth Press, 2010.

Sherman, Casey, *Animal: The Bloody Rise and Fall of the Mob's Most Feared Assassin*. Boston, Northeastern University Press, 2013.

Shea, John, *Rat Bastards: The South Boston Irish Mobster Who Took the Rap When Everyone Else Ran*, New York, HarperCollins Publishers, 2009.

Songini, Mark, *Boston Mob: The Rise and Fall of The New England Mob and Its Most Notorious Killer*, New York, St. Martin's Press, 2014.

Sweeney, Emily, *Gangland Boston: A Tour Through the Deadly Streets of Organized Crime*, Lyons Press, 2017.

Weeks, Kevin, and Phyllis Karas, *Brutal: The Untold Story of My Life Inside Whitey Bulger's Irish Mob*, New York, ReganBooks, An Imprint of HarperCollins Publishers, 2006.

Slaughter in the Streets is set in 9.5-point Palatino, which was designed by Hermann Zapf and released initially in 1949 by the Stempel foundry and later by other companies, most notably the Mergenthaler Linotype Company. Named after the sixteenth-century Italian master of calligraphy Giovanni Battista Palatino, Palatino is based on the humanist typefaces of the Italian Renaissance, and reflects Zapf's expertise as a calligrapher. Copyeditor for this project was Shannon LeMay-Finn. The book was designed by Brad Norr Design, Minneapolis, Minnesota, and typeset by Toppan Best-set Premedia Limited. Printed and manufactured by Maple Press on acid-free paper.

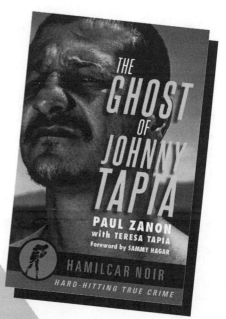

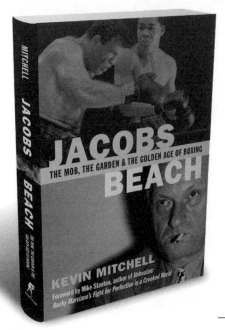

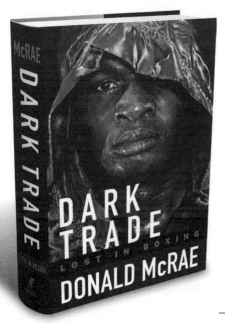

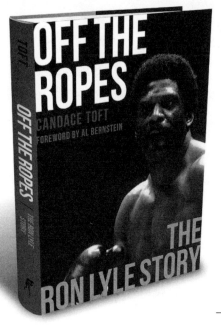

In her deeply researched biography of Denver's rugged contender, Candace Toft shows that Lyle's battles inside the ring, though dramatic, were mere shadows compared with the harrowing but ultimately redemptive journey of his life. Off the Ropes is a reminder that boxers, like the rest of us, have to keep fighting, even when the bright lights have gone down and the crowds gone home.

—**Paul Beston, author of**
The Boxing Kings: When American Heavyweights Ruled the Ring

O*ff the Ropes: The Ron Lyle Story* explores not only the greatest era of heavyweights in boxing history, but also tells an equally compelling personal tale. Ron Lyle grew up in the Denver projects, one of nineteen children in a tight-knit, religious family. At twenty, he was convicted for a disputed gang killing and served seven and a half years at the Colorado State Penitentiary at Cañon City, where he learned to box before he was paroled in 1969.

After a meteoric amateur career, he turned pro in 1971, and over the next seven years established an outstanding professional record, which, in addition to near misses versus Muhammad Ali and George Foreman, included a brutal knockout win over one of the era's most feared fighters, big-punching Earnie Shavers.

Then, in 1978, Lyle was indicted for murder a second time and, even though he was acquitted, his career was effectively over. The years that followed were filled with struggle, a captivating love story, and eventual redemption.

Off the Ropes: The Ron Lyle Story is the poignant, uplifting biography of a singular man.

Find *Off the Ropes* at your favorite bookstore or online retailer! Or order online at www.offtheropesbook.com.

9781949590012 | HARDCOVER | OCTOBER 2018

HAMILCAR
PUBLICATIONS
BOSTON